# Yearning
# for the Wind

# YEARNING FOR THE WIND

## CELTIC REFLECTIONS ON NATURE AND THE SOUL

# TOM COWAN

NEW WORLD LIBRARY
NOVATO, CALIFORNIA

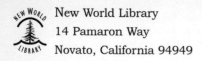 New World Library
14 Pamaron Way
Novato, California 94949

Front cover design by Mary Ann Casler
Text design and typography by Katie Blount

Library of Congress Cataloging-in-Publication Data
Cowan, Thomas Dale.
  Yearning for the wind : Celtic reflections on nature and the
soul / by Tom Cowan.
      p.   cm.
Includes index.
ISBN 1-57731-411-5 (pbk.)
1. Nature—Religious aspects. 2. Celts—Religion.
3.  Spiritual life.  I. Title.
BL435.C69 2003
299'.16—dc21                              2003002287

First Printing, June 2003
ISBN 1-57731-411-5
Printed in Canada on acid-free, partially recycled paper
Distributed to the trade by Publishers Group West

10  9  8  7  6  5  4  3

*This book is dedicated to all the*
*Shamanic Drumming Circles around the world*
*that inspire hope and healing for all of us.*

# Contents

FOREWORD
BY Sandra Ingerman   xi

ACKNOWLEDGMENTS
xv

INTRODUCTION
xvii

CHAPTER 1
Walking through Soul   1

CHAPTER 2
Mist, Flowers, and Southerly Wind   5

CHAPTER 3
Peepers, Figworts, and Baby Hawks   9

CHAPTER 4
A Source for Mystics   15

CHAPTER 5
Wading with Salmon   19

CHAPTER 6
Sacred Rivers   25

CHAPTER 7
The Love and Affection of the Moon   31

CHAPTER 8

THE WATERLESS WELL 35

CHAPTER 9

FORGIVE 39

CHAPTER 10

THE HIDDEN MOTHERS 43

CHAPTER 11

QUEEN MAEVE'S RULES FOR SOUL MAKING 47

CHAPTER 12

RUSH HOUR 51

CHAPTER 13

THE SHEEP AND THE GRAEL 57

CHAPTER 14

THE THREE HARPERS 63

CHAPTER 15

MOST THIS AMAZING DAY 67

CHAPTER 16

THE WINDS OF FATE 73

CHAPTER 17

TAKING CHARGE OF THE CENTER 77

CHAPTER 18

WALK IN TRUTH 83

CHAPTER 19

HOME RUNS IN A NEMETON 89

CHAPTER 20

CIRCLES OF MYSTERY 95

CHAPTER 21
The Big Bang of Divine Life  101

CHAPTER 22
The Shifting Shapes of God  105

CHAPTER 23
Night Watching  109

CHAPTER 24
Faeries Ohio Style  115

CHAPTER 25
Where Have All the Strawberries Gone?  121

CHAPTER 26
Fear and Love  125

CHAPTER 27
Nothing So Good Has Taken Their Place 129

CHAPTER 28
The Strength of Heaven  135

CHAPTER 29
A Haunting  139

CHAPTER 30
In the No-Beginning  143

CHAPTER 31
Yearning for the Wind  149

CHAPTER 32
The Coldest Beltane  153

CHAPTER 33
The Finest Music in All the World  159

CHAPTER 34
FACE EAST   163

CHAPTER 35
SKY TALK   167

CHAPTER 36
WHAT'S A HEAVEN FOR?   171

CHAPTER 37
SOUL STUFFING   175

CHAPTER 38
A RIDDLE   179

CHAPTER 39
HEALING THE GREAT SPLIT   183

CHAPTER 40
INVOKE LIFE!   187

ENDNOTES
191

INDEX
195

ABOUT THE AUTHOR
203

# Foreword

Once upon a time a spell was cast upon people across the land. The spell made people believe we are all separate beings with no connection to each other and no connection with nature or the rest of life. The spell continued with the belief that anything we could not see, hear, feel, smell, or taste with our ordinary senses did not exist. And the spell caused people to believe that only humans had a soul which a punishing God judged the nature of. Happiness only came from financial gain, collecting material objects, and having power over people, the animal world, and all of nature. The spell also set the belief that individuals were not creative and their role was to behave and conform to society.

The effect of this spell put people to sleep. They forgot about the beauty of life and their own soul's purpose. The light went out of people's eyes as the old knowledge of how to talk to nature was forgotten. Empty gazes and looks of fear and desperation replaced the light. The veils between the worlds closed down. Magical thinking was replaced by reductionistic thinking. The magic was gone along with people's souls. These were dark times indeed.

If this spell sounds familiar it should. It was cast upon the human race before our parents' lifetime. It has created great despair, violence toward each other, and a dishonoring of life and our environment.

Human beings are social creatures. We crave connection. Today on an unconscious level we crave to remember our connection to the moon, stars, sun, earth, air, water, animals, trees, plants, rocks, insects, birds, and reptiles. We want to remember we are part of continuing cycles and to return to the flow of the river of life and discontinue walking against it. We yearn for a time when the veils between the Other Worlds and ordinary reality open again and mystical pathways return between the human and nonhuman worlds.

This spell that has been cast throughout the world is very slowly starting to break. But those who are beginning to wake up are still in a stupor.

Tom Cowan in *Yearning for the Wind* provides a potion to break the spell. His words are delicious and fragrant and as we drink them in we remember the Truth. His interweaving of metaphors speaks to the very core of our being, cells, and soul. He reminds us how to retrieve our soul. His inspiring essays create an inner smile that as we continue reading reignites the spark in our eyes.

Some believe that shamans were the last people to speak to nature. Tom teaches us this old shamanic skill not by teaching techniques but by inspiring us to change our consciousness and create a new way of life that embraces harmony within and without.

The possibilities of reestablishing communication with nature and our souls and reconnecting with the cycles, rhythm, and flow of the river of life reminds us that the light we seek is not far away.

You will find yourself smiling as you read *Yearning for the Wind.* You will find the light returning to your eyes. You will awake from the spell cast upon you with gentle words leading you back to the Truth and a more meaningful way of living. Your soul will be fed on a very deep level.

I first met Tom Cowan at a workshop I was teaching in the late 1980s. At first I perceived Tom as a student of mine. In a very short time I saw him as a peer and a great teacher. He has a great sense of humor, a deep desire to experience new things, his mind is brilliant at making connections between things, and he is a person to whom people turn for knowledge and leadership. I have always honored Tom's integrity and his gentle spirit.

We have many students in common. There is such a palpable excitement from students who finish his teachings. His students cannot say enough good things about their experience with him and his work. He is a sane voice in the midst of a troubled world.

As you read *Yearning for the Wind* you will remember how to truly reach toward life. Enjoy!

Sandra Ingerman, author of
*Soul Retrieval* and *Medicine for the Earth*

# Acknowledgments

This book emerges from years of thinking about things, reading, praying, talking and traveling with all sorts of people, and basically allowing life to happen. So many people appear in my life at just the right moment when I need support, prodding, and restraint that I am not able to thank them all individually. But I thank daily the One who sends them.

I would like to especially thank the following co-walkers for encouraging me in my restless musings about things shamanic, Celtic, mystical, and fun.

Susan McClellan for reminding me that the shaman's search for meaning can always go deeper; Janine Ellison for bringing forth the dance that is always present in soul making; Jodie von Gal for reminding me that resiliency is both sacred and secular; Colleen Cannon for living a life of sacred service rooted in a sacred scape of land; Frank MacEowen for teachings that are young, vibrant, and very old; Karl Schlotterbeck for standing firm in the ways of Druidry and showing me how to do that; Gabriel Ross for reminding me that some goddesses are blond and wear black tuxedos; Susan Lee Cohen, my agent, who has supported both my writing and non-writing escapades over many years; Ruth Aber for keeping the wind ever at our backs; Sandra Ingerman for her vision of the soul's power and worth; and last but not least, Michael Harner for his faith in shamanism as a perennial response to human problems, questions, and joys.

I want to thank also the following people at New World Library: my editor Georgia Hughes for seeing the possibilities in this manuscript, having faith in it, and bringing it to fulfillment; copy editor Mike Ashby for his wise and prudent insights for polishing the text; and designer Mary Ann Casler for a terrific book cover.

And special thanks to Jack Maguire for being steadfast, for being Buddhist in the midst of Celtic craziness, and for being there.

# Introduction

*Sometimes I go around feeling sorry for myself,*
*but all the while I am carried by the wind*
*across the sky.*

— from the Chippewa

Celtic artwork is braided, entwined, knotted with loops of mystery and magic. Everything seems to fold onto something else, as well as back onto itself. The tongue of a bird twists and turns its way around the borders of a scene to become the tail of some other animal. One beast's claw becomes another's paw. You get the feeling that birds, beasts, humans, trees, and plants share a mystical understanding that nothing is separate, that all is one. You get the feeling that this is the way things are supposed to be.

The poet Amergin sang the following lines when he led the original Gaelic tribes from the Iberian Peninsula to Ireland:

*I invoke the land of Ireland:*
*Forceful, the fertile sea;*
*Fertile, the lush higlands;*
*Lush, the showery woods;*
*Showery, the river of waterfalls;*
*Of waterfalls, the lake of deep-pools;*
*Deep-pooled, the hilltop well;*
*Welling, the people of gatherings;*
*Gathering, the tribes of Tara;*
*I invoke the Land of Ireland.*[1]

Although my version takes some liberties with the original, the overlapping of lines and images is true to the way Amergin chanted this poem eons ago as he put the braiding of Celtic art into song.

*Yearning for the Wind* is a book of braided chapters that, like the lines in Amergin's song, overlap and lead into one another. Sometimes the tongue of one chapter turns out to be the tail of another. What the book is about is the interplay of soul and nature, and how that playing creates mystical pathways between the human and nonhuman worlds in which we live. When we are alert to this dynamic, we more fully realize the wondrous intimacy between the human world and the natural world around us.

Mystics and shamans have long recognized that consciousness pervades all created things, what the Lakota holy man Black Elk called "the shapes of all things in the spirit, and the shape of all shapes as they must live together like one being."[2] The great spiritual teachers of every continent and century have confirmed this inter-dependence of ordinary and non-ordinary realities, the marriage of heaven and earth, or as I like to think of it, the oneness of soul and nature. And as soul and nature inform our lives with greater immediacy, we become better prepared to engage in the great purpose of life, which the English poet John Keats called "soul-making."[3]

These short, braided chapters are little windows into the mysteries of nature and soul, small meditations on how Spirit is present in our everyday lives. They are small invitations to encourage you to realize your own soul's intimacy with the world around you. They are meant to make you wonder.

Very little in this book has been changed to protect the innocent, or the wicked for that matter. The people and events are real. I would not alter one of them. They are all currents in that great wind that carries my soul across the sky.

## CHAPTER 1

# WALKING THROUGH SOUL

When I walk through the woods, I end up talking to myself. No, not end up. The internal dialogue usually begins within the first few minutes. I make plans, fret, scold myself or others, review arguments I lost, occasionally outline my deepest thoughts for some real or imagined presentation. It's not always useless chatter, but it distracts me and I fail to notice the gnarled oaks, the boulders with craggy faces, the sudden rock outcrops with dramatic views of the river, the mountains in the distance, the clearings.

I will discover myself standing on a magnificent rocky outcrop, talking incessantly to myself about the best time to wax my car or wondering what it would be like to live in a culture that had no word for time. Then I suddenly become aware of the magnificent view before me and realize how totally oblivious I was to the beauties and powers of nature, which are the very reason I walk in the woods in the first place.

Nature, however, always finds some way to interrupt my internal chatter. She'll trip me on a root, or turn my foot on a stone, or swipe my eye with a low-hanging branch, and I'll remember. But within minutes, I forget again, jaunting on as if the woods were not really there, as if resolving to wax my car before winter were more important.

I should really be better at hiking in the woods. I have been hiking in the woods since before I could walk. My parents took me into the Missouri Ozarks when I was a baby who still viewed the woods — and everything around me — as part of me. Of course, like all growing children, I stopped seeing the world this way. We all do. We create the Great Split between ourselves and nature, thinking we are different, or removed, or even alien to the natural world. I must have done a good job of it because I can spend hours in the woods and never get out of my own head.

There are many spiritual practices that attempt to remove this dualism of the Me and the Not-Me and to recover and strengthen that sense of wholeness and oneness that we knew intuitively as children. I have tried many of these over the years with varying success. Clearly I am not an expert at it.

Of course, we don't ever really lose this sense of oneness with nature. We still shudder in delight at a sunset behind the mountains, catch our breath seeing the change of light on the river, and thrill to the ever-moving cloud patterns sweeping the sky. In such moments, we know that there really is no duality in all this, that on some mystical level we are the river and the setting sun, we are the clouds above the hills. But our internal chatter, like some inner demon who despises mysticism, derails those moments of magic and grace.

In a medieval document known as *The Four Ancient Books of Wales,* the Welsh Druid and mystic Taliesin says: "I adore my God, my Strengthener, who infused through my head a Soul to direct me with its seven faculties: fire, earth, water, air, mist, flowers, and southerly wind."[4] Sometimes I try to recite this as I hike through the woods, to hold this vision that the elements through which I walk are the powers of my soul. If only I could always be hiking this Great Mystery: assured that the hills, rivers, trees, and clouds are the faculties of my soul extended beyond my head, my body, my feet, even beyond the footprints I leave in the dust of the trail behind me.

My soul can hike farther than I can, if my thinking mind will only give it free rein. The twelfth-century German mystic Hildegard of Bingen would have said that my soul could hike on forever. She put it this way: "Just as the heart is hidden in the human body, so is the body surrounded by the powers of the soul because these reach to the ends of the earth."[5]

To the ends of the earth!

I don't tote my soul through the woods as if it were an uncomfortable backpack. My soul carries me. Along trails, up cliffs, down to the river, to the far mountains, to the setting sun, beyond the wisps of cloud turning pink in the west. Air, fire, water, earth, mist, flowers, and southerly wind. These are the stuff of soul.

It is not the woods I hike through. I hike through the field of power around me that I call my soul, even though at this moment, in this place, I may call it "the woods."

When I walk through the woods, I end up scolding myself for being so oblivious to trees, air, rocks, river, my soul.

# CHAPTER 2

# Mist, Flowers, and Southerly Wind

Mist, flowers, and southerly wind. How did these three acquire the same status as earth, air, fire, and water?

Mist is air and water. Southerly wind is air and heat. Flowers are a spectacular blend of soil, water, sunlight — and even air, for a flower does not stop at the edge of its skin, any more than we stop at the edge of ours. Around every flower is the sweet fragrance of scented air. This field of fragrance is the flower's soul. The soul is not just inside the flower. The flower lives inside its soul. As we do.

As a child I used to obsess about the riddle that asks: If a tree falls in a forest, and there is no one to hear it, does it make any sound? I always suspected that both answers — yes and no — were wrong, or not quite right, and that the science of sound waves and eardrums missed some important point.

The same riddle might apply to flowers. If there is no one around to sniff it, does a flower still smell fragrant? If no one believes in the souls of flowers, do they still have souls? I would answer "yes" to both questions. There is no stopping the sweet fragrance of flowers. It is part of the "grandeur of God," which poet Gerard Manley Hopkins says "will flame out like shining from shook foil."[6]

There's no stopping the soul that radiates out and around us, anymore than one can stop the sweet perfume of a rose. You could, of course, hold your nose. But the rose will continue to exude its rich fragrance even while you suffocate.

The soul is not in the body, the body is in the soul. This is not easy to understand or to live. But we must try. If we don't, we circumscribe our life and greatly reduce the ways we know our souls, we strengthen the Great Split between us and creation.

Mist, flowers, and southerly wind defy the distinctions and dualities of the elements by reminding us that the elements merge and flow into each other like Celtic braid work. Each of these three is a combination of elements, with air being the one common to all. Is this because air, like soul, is always both in and around us?

An Irish text from the tenth century called *The*

*Evernew Tongue* purports to be a teaching by the apostle Philip concerning creation and the nature of the universe. It states, "Every material and every element and every nature which is seen in the world are all combined . . . in the body of every human person."[7] It then goes on to explain this specifically. Wind and air are our breath; heat and boiling from fire make the blood; the sun and stars put luster in people's eyes; bitterness and saltiness cause tears and the anger in human hearts; stones and clay are our flesh, bones, and limbs; flowers and other beautiful colors of the earth give complexion to our faces and cheeks. All of these are "in the body of every human person."

The elements of nature are not just out there, or in our souls, but in our bodies as well.

A Welsh document called *The Book of Llanrwst* offers a similar description of how all the elements of creation are present in the human body, and, adding two, describes what it calls "the eight parts of man." "The seventh is the Holy Ghost, from whom issues the soul and life; and the eighth is Christ, that is, the intellect, wisdom, and the light of soul and life."[8] The physical elements of nature, soul, life, intellect, wisdom, and the mysterious "light of soul and life" — these are what we are.

What it boils down to is this. We are mist, flowers, and southerly wind. We are composites of all we see around us. We have the woods, river, clouds, mountains within our very bodies, and in some unexplainable way, these elements that make up the physical universe and our physical bodies are also the powers of our souls.

Try this the next time some natural scene of beauty or power pulls you toward it. It might be a radiant sunset, the stars on a very clear, cold night, a great expanse of beach with waves rolling in one after another, or just a small creek trickling over mossy stones. Close your eyes and continue to see the scene, and realize that the pull it has on you is coming from within you as much as from without. The pulling, the longing to let it fill you, the yearning to know the sublime nature of this scene reside in both you and the scene itself. There is no barrier between you and it. Even though it seems to be "out there," or even "way out there," it is in your soul. It is part of your soul, for there is no "way out there." Its elements are your body, pulling, longing, and yearning. The whole Earth is pulling, longing, and yearning. Take a deep breath and let these wonders fill you. Then open your eyes again.

When you leave this scene, all the glory, beauty, and power of it will go with you. They are in your soul. You are still walking beneath those stars, along that beach, before that sunset. When you later hear that stream splashing over the mossy stones, you will not be hearing it just inside your head. It is out there. Out there in your soul.

Yes, there is always a great and terrible crashing when any tree falls, for no tree falls that does not fall within my soul.

# CHAPTER 3

# Peepers, Figworts, and Baby Hawks

One spring day I was hiking down Bull Hill, a mountain north of Cold Spring, New York, on the Hudson River. As I turned a bend in the trail, I stumbled upon two young women whom I immediately suspected were from New York City. They were decked out in new, crisp, clean designer clothing. They looked like they had just stepped out of a catalogue of mock safari outfits.

The women had stopped by a vernal pool that would be dry by July or August. Each year I love to stop at this very spot, for it is high on the mountain yet swampy enough to be a mating ground for tree frogs. The mating song of the tree frogs is intense, mesmerizing, and can bring on altered states of consciousness if you give yourself to it. It carries all the juice and excitement of springtime and wet, new life.

The women seemed startled when they saw me; they responded somewhat nervously, as if they felt the need to explain what they were doing on the trail. They acted as if they had wandered onto private land and were afraid of trespassing.

Or I may have startled them out of a somewhat different state of consciousness as I lumbered into their soul space.

"Oh!" one of the women exclaimed. She looked at me with an embarrassed laugh but with the shrewd glance of a wary New Yorker scoping the danger level that my presence created.

"We were just listening to the chirping from all these baby hawks," the other said, coming to her rescue with an equally nervous laugh.

Baby hawks! I suppressed a smile. If this chirping was indeed from baby hawks, there were a hundred thousand of them! And every predator in the Hudson Valley would be swooping in from all directions for a feast! Nature does not allow vulnerable baby birds to announce their exact location so shrilly.

"Do you think they just recently hatched?" the second woman asked eagerly, trying to engage me in conversation.

I'm usually reluctant to destroy fantasies, but this felt like a moment of truth, so I said, "Well, I hate to say this, but I don't think those are baby hawks. They're tree frogs. We call them peepers. They chirp like that for a few weeks every spring while they're mating."

I expected to see their faces fall in disappointment, but they were tough, resilient New Yorkers. Their eyes actually lit up even more brightly. They gasped in delighted surprise.

"Peepers! Mating frogs!" one of them said, excitedly grabbing the other by the arm. "Just think of it! We're actually here the week they're getting it on!"

"Perfect timing!" agreed her companion. "How romantic! They're very loud."

"Yes," I said, not sharing their enthusiasm. "We actually like it when the good times end, so we can sleep at night."

The two both squinted at me in incomprehension. "You mean you can't sleep when they're having sex?" This was a new world for them.

"The noise," I explained. "They chirp like that all night."

"And you can actually hear them in the night?" She didn't seem able to visualize anyone sleeping so close to raw, unbridled lovemaking in the natural world. Or she didn't realize there were other pools of water like this one closer to home where the same ancient mating ritual was going on. Perhaps she herself lived on the fortieth floor in an Upper East Side apartment building where even the wailing of emergency sirens doesn't penetrate.

"Yeah. We hear them."

"How romantic!" They looked at each other mischievously.

I may have destroyed one fantasy, but at least I replaced it with another. I wished the two women an enjoyable day, and continued my descent.

Once there was a hermit living on the edge of a lake in Ireland. One morning he woke up and thought how nice it would be to have a fish for breakfast. So he got in his boat and rowed out to the center of the lake. As he did so, he noticed the hermit who lived on the other side of the lake walking right across the water. He could not believe his eyes! When they got within speaking distance, the first hermit shouted, "What are you doing out here?"

The second hermit answered, "I just thought I'd come out here and pick some flowers for my altar. But what are you doing rowing your boat across this meadow?"

Taken aback and a bit confused, the first hermit answered awkwardly, "Well, uh . . . well, I thought I would come out and, you know, see if I could catch a fish for breakfast."

"Oh," said the second hermit with a smile of approval. "I think they're biting over by that clump of figworts."

So the first hermit thanked him, rowed over to the figwort bushes, lowered his line, and sure enough, caught a splendid fish.

He went home and had a delicious breakfast. And the other hermit went back with a beautiful bouquet of flowers for his altar.

I often think about those two women from New York when I think about those hermits.

Maybe they had indeed heard the chirping of baby hawks. There are many places in my soul that I have yet to discover.

CHAPTER 4

# A Source for Mystics

Every day we must rely on our senses to get us through our rounds of activities, even though we are repeatedly told that our senses can deceive us. Yet fully warned, people still live according to the old adage, "Seeing is believing."

I often wonder why we don't also claim, "Hearing is believing." When it comes to belief, we tend to favor our eyes over our ears and other senses. Maybe we don't trust our ears because they are more skillful deceivers than our eyes. Ears, after all, can lure us into a nursery of baby hawks. Worse, the limitations of hearing might convince us that a tree falls silently in the distance or that people across the street are moving their lips but not really talking. On the other hand, what are we to make of hermits walking on water and rowing boats across meadows of flowers? Seeing is believing.

In an old Irish myth, the hero Cormac journeys to the Land of Truth in the Otherworld, where he is instructed in the mystical realities of the Universe. There he sees a pool of water surrounded by hazel trees that drop their nuts into the water. Five salmon break open the nuts to eat the kernels. The juice from the purple hazels colors the water, which then flows from the pool in five streams that disappear beyond the horizon. Cormac inquires about this strange scene.

The ruler of this enchanted land, Manannan mac Lir, explains that the hazels are the Nuts of Wisdom, the fish are the Salmon of Wisdom, and the five streams, carrying the juice from the nuts and flowing from the pool, are our five senses. Then he tells Cormac, "Everyone drinks from the five streams. But only mystics, poets, and people with the gift of vision drink from the five streams *and the pool itself.*"

I have been trying to put this difficult truth about reality into practice for many years. It is truly revolutionary in terms of the accepted paradigm in our society that says the objects of our senses are just physical objects. According to Manannan, the information that comes through our senses comes with otherworldly wisdom from the Land of Truth. Physical reality is not just physical, it is spiritual; it comes from a place of truth, wisdom, and sacred knowledge.

This means that a tree is more than a tree, a rock more than a rock, a drop of rain more than a drop of rain. Even a pile of garbage, an automobile wreck, the atrocities on the evening news — all of these are not just events in ordinary reality. A lake may not be only a lake, or a meadow simply a meadow of flowers. Everything is a stream of consciousness flowing from nonordinary reality. To believe that this other reality is just as real as the one we experience daily through our senses takes faith, or as Cormac learned, it takes mysticism, poetry, and visionary gifts.

The People of Vision drink from the streams of their senses and the pool itself. They know that what they see, hear, smell, taste, touch, and feel convey supernatural meaning that is more eternal and soul-full than the physical reality that is most apparent.

Perhaps the ability of the senses to trick us is actually a reminder about this. Rather than "failing" to represent reality accurately, the occasional deception might actually be a call to remind us that the purely physical sensations that come from the outer world to our inner world are not what they seem because they are always *much more* than what they seem.

On a trip to Vienna, where I taught a seminar in Celtic shamanism, my Austrian host, Paul, noticed as we rode the elevator up to my hotel room that my luggage still had the airline flight tags on it. He reached down and said, "We will take these off. They will be a source for mystics."

As he began to tear them from the handles of my

suitcases, I wondered how exactly that would work. "What do you mean?" I asked.

"You will attract mystics!" Paul repeated, sounding very assured that he understood the problem, even though I hadn't the foggiest idea of how that would happen.

"How will those tags attract mystics?"

Paul looked at me askance. Then, enunciating more slowly and with greater pains to soften his German accent, he said carefully and clearly, "Not mystics. Mistakes."

"*Mißverständnis!*" I announced proudly, my college German courses paying off. "Mistakes."

"Yes," he agreed. "There will be mistakes."

"Well, take them off," I said, "but it would be nice to be a source for mystics."

"Ah, it would be very nice to be a source for mystics," he agreed.

We rode up the rest of the way to my floor, silently, both pondering the joy of being a source for mystics.

Mistakes. We ought to value them. They are a source for mystics.

# CHAPTER 5

# Wading with Salmon

I never swam with dolphins, but I waded with salmon. It was late October and I was spending a few days with my friends Peg and Don in the cabin they built themselves on the south fork of the Yaquina River. Their home is located on the western slope of Oregon's Coast Ranges, where salmon return in late autumn to the mountain streams where they were spawned.

Peg loaned me Don's pair of rubber waders, and we sloshed out into the river just a few feet from her kitchen door. The day was bright and warm, crisp as autumn should be, and within minutes I saw the first of several long sleek salmon swishing and twisting their way upstream. I stood still, hushed, in awe of this prehistoric rite that has been going on longer than human beings have walked on Earth. Then one brushed against my leg! I had never been so close to creatures of such powerful myth and mystery. The Salmon of Wisdom right at my feet.

The fish were not beautiful, however. Their skin had sickly yellow splotches, the mealy discoloration that revealed the true purpose of their journey. They were coming home to die.

"Can't eat 'em this late in the year," said Peg, somewhat glumly. "They're rotting."

It's fitting that they come home in late October, for according to an old Irish belief, the souls that die each year must wait till the feast of Samhain, or what we call Halloween, before they can cross over into the Otherworld. This is the "night outside of time," the old Celtic New Year, November Eve, a weird night in neither the old year nor the new one. A crack between the worlds.

My partner Jack's father died some years ago on Halloween. He timed it perfectly. He was Irish. Earlier the same year, my maternal grandmother died, but it was February. She had a few months to wait. She was German.

Waiting to go somewhere after death is a universal idea, I suppose, but at odds with the reply a mystic once gave to the question "Where do souls go when they die?" He answered, "No place."

Our souls stretch to the ends of the earth, according to Hildegard of Bingen. Possibly beyond the ends of

the Earth. In some ways, we may not have to go anywhere because we have never left. Like the salmon who
return to the headwaters where they cracked their first
nut, we might even now be in that same continuous,
uninterrupted flowing of life that encircles the Earth
and into which we are born and in which we will die. It
is only our restless minds and egos that go swimming
hither and thither through the short years of our lives,
never knowing that they swim through the currents of
our souls.

Our souls are still connected to the Source from
which we came and in which we will once again be har-
bored after death. We needn't look back for we have
never left.

That night Peg made a large batch of mashed potatoes, as is her Irish custom and as it was that of her
Irish grandmothers. Now an Irish grandmother herself,
she wondered if we should put some of the "tatties" on
the gatepost for the faeries. After all, it was Halloween.

"But, Peg, you don't have a gate," I objected. It's
true, there are no gates on their land. Life can come
and go freely as it pleases.

"Well, we could use the posts on the footbridge."
She was referring to the narrow bridge Don had built
across a small stream diverted from the river that
makes a kind of island on which their cabin sits.
"Faeries can't be beggars or choosers . . . even though
they are."

It was decided. We would smear potatoes on the
bridge.

But the best-laid plans on November Eve can go awry.

We ate dinner and then watched a video of River-dance, an Irish dance company that was taking the country by storm. We gabbed far into the night. And we drank too much Jameson's. We retired well after midnight with the pot of mashed potatoes still sitting on the stove growing cold.

The next morning I came down from the bus that serves as Peg and Don's "guest cabin." It's an ancient, converted school bus rigged up with a hot plate, a woodstove, and what you could call a bed. It sits a ways up the river from their cabin. I was hungry. As I entered the cabin, I could smell something cooking. "What's for breakfast?" I asked.

"Mashed potatoes!" Peg answered devilishly.

Then I remembered. I had completely forgotten our plan to put potatoes on the bridge posts. "Do you think we could still do it?" I asked.

"What's time to the faeries?" Peg grabbed the pot, two wooden spoons, and we headed out.

As we spread potatoes on the bridge, I suddenly heard a loud sloshing in the river, getting closer. Some-thing big. I turned to look and saw a man in an official-looking uniform, wearing waders and trudging knee-deep up the river. Peg squinted at him and muttered under her breath to me, "Fish and Game Commission. Comes every year to count salmon."

The salmon counter stopped a few feet below us and wished us a good morning. We returned the greeting.

Peg chatted while I continued to spoon spuds onto the bridge post.

"How's the count this year?"

"'Bout the same...," he drawled, his eyes glazing distractedly as he squinted at our potatoes.

"As last year," Peg finished for him, when he didn't seem inclined to elaborate.

"Same as always," he mumbled. He continued to stare at the mashed potatoes for a moment, then blinked as if remembering why he was standing in the river and said, "Well, I don't want to keep you folks. Your potatoes might get cold."

"Nor we you," added Peg cheerfully. "Salmon get away from you."

He tipped his cap, turned in the water, and sloshed upstream, clicking his counter. He never looked back.

# CHAPTER 6

# SACRED RIVERS

Rivers are mysterious beings. The Cherokee call a river "the Great Long Person." I grew up on the banks of the mighty Mississippi, called the "Father of Waters" by Native American people and "Ol' Man River" by composer Jerome Kern. The Lenape in the Hudson Valley call the river Mahi-cani-tok, the "River That Flows in Two Directions." A fjord, the Hudson changes with the tides. Irish legends say that a person who drinks water from the Boyne River in June will become a seer and a poet. I've done that, but I don't let on that I have.

Heraclitus believed that a person can never step into the same river twice. If he's right, then salmon coming home at the end of their lives do not really re-turn to the same river in which they were born. Or do they? Don't these same old rivers just keep rollin' along?

Whenever I sit by a river or swim in one, I feel like I have returned to some spiritual source, a strong, eter-nal presence in my life that is always the same, no mat-ter how the waters swell or recede as the seasons come and go, and the rains and melting snows flood the banks. A river always feels like a realm of the Eternal here on Earth, flowing, changing, yes, but somehow al-ways the same, always there.

A legend from the Missouri Ozarks relates that the Creator told the Osage people there, "I have not made these rivers and streams for nothing. I have made them so you will have a means to reach old age." Perhaps that is why rivers and streams are there, and why we love them.

In Indo-European cultures, we hear about sacred rivers having their sources in the Otherworld. The Ganges in India, for example, originates in a realm of Paradise called the Land of Truth. The ancient Celts who lived along the lower Danube named this river after the goddess Danu, whose name means "waters from heaven." In Ireland both the Shannon and the Boyne originate in the Pool of Hazelnuts, Salmon, and Wisdom that Cormac discovered in the Land of Truth. It appears that from India to Ireland there is a wide-spread understanding that a sacred river brings knowl-edge, power, and wisdom from a Place of Truth that lies beyond the everyday world of the senses.

When the old Irish gods, known as the Tuatha De Danann, learned that another race of humans was about to invade Ireland, their Druids decided to hide the Pool of Wisdom. They removed it from ordinary reality and sealed it up in the Otherworld so that mortals would not find the water or misuse its power.

Shannon, however, a granddaughter of the god Lir, discovered the hiding place and broke the Druidic enchantment. Her motives are unclear. Some accounts say that she sought revenge for being slighted by other gods and goddesses. Some tales say she simply wanted to enhance her own divine qualities with the wisdom from the sacred pool.

But when Shannon violated the Druids' spell in order to attain that power, the water itself roared, rose up, and chased her back into the physical landscape. She fled swiftly across the length of Ireland as the waters pursued her, and the path of her escape became the riverbed for the great River Shannon. Some say the waters drowned her and she was never heard from again. Others say something different. She *became* those waters, and she still flows across the land, now one of Ireland's two sacred rivers.

The Boyne had similar origins. The goddess Boann was married to Nechtain, the god in charge of guarding the Pool of Wisdom in the Otherworld. Desiring the water's secrets, Boann followed Nechtain one night when he went to perform his protective rituals at the pool. She discovered its location and observed the secret rite. When her husband left, she stepped forward and performed the ritual that she hoped would reveal the water and its powers, but she failed to perform it correctly.

Offended, the water rose up and chased Boann across Ireland, and it became the river named after her, the Boyne.

There are echoes of Eve in these stories. Pandora, too. A supposedly "troublesome" female violates a sacred taboo in order to learn, to understand, to be enriched with the wisdom of the Otherworld. But could these stories be more ancient than the versions we currently know? Could there be an even older story, now long lost, about the folly of trying to remove the sacred knowledge of the universe and to withhold the secret wisdom of creation from ordinary reality?

Shannon, Boann, Pandora, Eve. Could these be local names for some heroic, primal goddess who defied the ancient taboos and released the Wisdom of the Otherworld so that it might flow through ordinary reality and enlighten men and women struggling to make sense of their senses? Perhaps these ancestral Mothers birthed into being the pain, sorrow, joy, love, and beauty that give meaning to our lives. For what the sacred literature of all cultures tells us is that the seemingly ordinary realities of our lives, whether good or bad, are the elements of Wisdom, the elements for soul making. By drinking from the Pool of Wisdom that flows into our world through ordinary daily events, we become "like gods," that is we become more certain of the divine qualities out of which we were created.

If you check a map of Ireland, you quickly see that the Shannon and Boyne do not have the same source, even though the myths say they both originate in the Pool of Wisdom. The Pool of Wisdom is not on any ordinary map. This is probably true of all rivers: we don't really know where they come from. They are just water that keeps on rollin' along, never to pass by again.

The next time you stand at the source of a river or even at a small spring bubbling up from the earth, ask the water, "Where do you really come from?" Perhaps it will tell you.

And why are some rivers sacred and some not? That is a trick question, meant to mislead you. All rivers are sacred.

CHAPTER 7

# THE LOVE AND AFFECTION
# OF THE MOON

E verything has spirit, soul, personality, and can communicate. Or so say the shamans of most indigenous cultures. Each culture has its own way of explaining these mysteries, what they signify, and what the ramifications are for human beings.

Every culture except ours, of course. The notion that there are spirits in all created things is not one of our favorite ideas. But it used to be. Up until the seventeenth century, Europeans believed in what might be called Christian animism. Theologians wrote and spoke about the Anima Mundi, the Soul of the World; and most people in all walks of life believed there were faeries and earth spirits in nature and spirits of the dead haunting various places.

But Protestant Reformers objected to this Catholic view as too pagan and superstitious, and the new scientists of that century began to doubt whether the physical world, including even animals, had consciousness or souls. The Western world soon lost faith in the spirit and soul of creation.

The Gaelic languages, however, still reflect this older worldview, possibly because the Gaelic-speaking regions of Ireland and Scotland were remote, rural, and not heavily influenced by the modern world until recently.

The Irish word for "nature" is *dúlra,* which contains the stem *dúil,* meaning "element" or "created thing." This root word is the first syllable in the Irish word for Creator: Dúileamh (pronounced "dool-yev" and always spelled with a capital *D).*

What is fascinating is that Dúileamh does not contain the root word for "create." There is another word for that. It also does not contain the word for God. Or Father. Or Almighty. Or Supreme. The most basic translation for Dúileamh would be something like the "Being of the Elements" or the "One Who Is in the Elements" or the "One Who *Is* the Elements."

Could it be that the life, consciousness, and soul of every created thing is the One Who Is in Them — the Dúileamh?

Even more intriguing is another meaning for *dúil.* This facile Irish noun can also mean "desire," "fondness," "expectation," or "hope."

Try thinking about all this for awhile.

Several curious questions may occur to you: Who is fond of whom? What is fond of what? Who desires whom... or what? What or who hopes, expects, yearns... and for what? for whom? Caught in this web of elements, nature, and created things, the most logical explanation is that the Creator longs for creation and is fond of creation, even as creation longs for the Creator and is fond of the Creator. Created things long for each other and are fond of each other in some mysterious way. We are caught in a crazy web of fondness, affection, yearning, and expectation. Everything yearns for everything! If we took this seriously, we might go mad!

An old Gaelic blessing says, "You are the pure love of the moon, you are the pure love of the stars, you are the pure love of the sun... and the dew... and the rain... and (finally) you are the pure love of each living creature."[9] The Scottish Highlanders bless each other with expressions like these: "The love and affection of the moon be yours, the love and affection of the sun be yours, the love and affection of the stars be yours," and on and on, including other natural elements until: "The love and affection of *each living creature* be yours."[10] It strains our modern sensibilities, and triggers our calloused cynicism, to entertain the thought that we live in a loving and affectionate universe. Imagine how your life would change if you believed this.

Imagine how you would have to change your life if you believed this.

The Elements. The Love and Affection of the Elements. The Pure Love of the Elements. The Being-of-the-Elements. The One-Who-Is-the-Elements.

Once in a workshop on Celtic shamanism, we were considering these Gaelic words, and a woman in the group sighed, "Oh, I wish our culture had words like these." Another participant quickly responded, "Wouldn't it be great if our culture had *ideas* like these?"

# CHAPTER 8

# The Waterless Well

There is a tradition in Ireland that if you offend a holy well, the water will move. It sort of packs up and goes somewhere else. You can offend a well by washing your clothes there, throwing trash into it, or depriving people of access if it is on your property.

A story is told that in County Tipperary, a parson was upset by the rambunctiousness of a group of young people who celebrated Garlic Sunday on the last weekend in July at a holy well on his property. So after they left, he posted a Keep Out sign. The water in the well stopped flowing. Later it bubbled up nearby, but safely off the parson's land. The new location, however, brought the well no peace. A local woman washed her clothes in it, so the spring moved once again, about a mile away, to its present site.

Nature demands our respect.

A holy well not far from the sixth-century monastery of Clonmacnoise on the banks of the Shannon River has dried up in recent years. An interpreter and guide at the monastery, who researched the well and wrote a thesis on it, points out that there is evidence that people have lived in the region since the Bronze Age. It is possible that this humble spring provided water for countless generations of human beings. So why did the well suddenly dry up?

The European Union has sent experts to Ireland (and other countries) to help farmers become more efficient. Their recommendation was to drain the swampy water in the area to make the land more arable. They did so, and the well went dry. The water may have stopped flowing because of modern hydrological experiments. But you can't help wondering if maybe there aren't personal reasons also. At any rate, over the last few years the water has not returned.

But that hasn't discouraged people from returning to honor the waterless well. They still come and tie clooties, or prayer strips, to the branches of the thorn tree that grows out of the well. Although, the same guide at the monastery claims that a local priest unties them and throws them away after the people leave to discourage the practice. She points out, however, that his sabotage is not working.

On a recent tour to Ireland, a dozen of us went off to search for the well. Following directions given us by the guide, we found the well about a fifteen-minute walk down the road in a field of cows. The thorn tree had just finished blooming; the stone walls of the well were cool and dark in the shade; and the three sacred stones, including one with the face of St. Ciaran, were still standing around the well. The cows began milling over toward us as we approached to see what we were up to, eyeing us with curiosity and suspicion.

And yes, there were a few weathered strips of cloth tied to the lower branches of the tree that had somehow escaped the priest's detection. They flapped in the wind as gentle reminders of the devout people who had brought to this holy place their *dúile:* their desires, fondness, expectations, and hopes.

Since the purpose of our tour was to honor ancient sites with prayers and rituals, we sat around the well, sang songs, prayed, and shook rattles reverently to honor the spirits there. We walked the circuit three times around the stones, kissed them, and finally tore strips from a blue bandanna, blessed them, and tied them to the tree with our prayers. We spent about an hour there in prayer, reflection, and meditation.

The idea that the water and the land might have love and affection for us and our activities gave us a keen sense of obligation. We felt a deep respect for this place where people have lived since time out of mind. In whatever ways we could, we expressed our gratitude for water in all its forms. We wondered if the spirit of the water that once flowed here minded being diverted to other fields by the EU's agricultural experts. Would the water ever return to the stone well if enough people visited it, prayed, walked the circuit around the stones, kissed them, and left their best wishes tied to the gnarled branches of the tree?

Would the water ever come back?

We finished up our visit and walked back to the monastery, deeply aware that we had participated in a rite that human beings have found important since earliest times. We had honored a sacred place.

Back at the interpretive center, some of our party went immediately to the lavatories and discovered "Closed" signs on the doors. The water level had dropped at the center during the previous hour that we had been honoring it down the road at the well. Had the water left the monastery to join us down the road? I don't know. All we can say is that the lavatories were temporarily closed to the public . . . until the water returned.

# CHAPTER 9

# FORGIVE

A shaman's power to heal, comfort, read omens, and serve her or his community in various ways comes from personal relationships with helping spirits. Some of these are the spirits of nature and the elements — the very landscape in which the shaman lives and works. Staying on good terms with these spirits requires prayer, ritual, sacrifice, and an attitude of humility — the kind of attitude that inspires us to ask the spirits to take pity on us human beings who have such difficulty making the right choices and living harmoniously with each other and the Earth.

In our own spiritual practice it is wise to acknowledge the land, rivers, fields, and resources that we depend upon: the water from clouds, rivers, and wells; the sunlight that cheers us and brings the warmth needed for growth; the wood and oil we burn; the meat and vegetables we eat; the stones, minerals, and plants we transform into useful materials for our homes and cities. It is wise to be ever mindful that these powers deserve our care, our deepest feelings, our respect.

The spirits of nature recognize their own role of service in the greater whole. After all, they are created, as we are, to serve others. Most of the time, they willingly submit to our needs. Sometimes not. A Native American expression after a disappointing hunt is, "The deer would not die for me today." We can only wonder why. Why, on certain days and nights, in certain seasons, does nature not cooperate?

In our role as participants and caretakers of nature's bounty, we can regularly express the gratitude and respect we owe the land and the great consciousness that ensouls it, the Divine Mystery behind these gifts. We can live, care for, and use the Earth's powers in ways that acknowledge their holiness.

One way to do this is to ask the spirits for forgiveness for the times we act thoughtlessly and heartlessly, and to ask forgiveness for people who never know the spirits in the natural world they take for granted or even misuse.

Here is a formula for acknowledging our faults based on a prayer attributed to St. Ciaran, who founded the monastery at Clonmacnoise. The refrain "Forgive" can also include "Thanks" for the healing powers of nature, the omens the universe presents to guide our way through life, and the many daily moments of beauty and joy from the natural world that enrich our lives.

You can address the prayer to any divine being or helping spirit. I have addressed it to the mothering spirits of the land and elements that the Celtic peoples in Roman times referred to simply as "The Mothers."

*Mothers of Life,*
> *you bless the Earth that gives us food,*
> *shelter, clothing, and tools for our*
> *work and play, and that provides*
> *the many paths that lead us*
> *through life,*
> > *Forgive.*

*Mothers of Life,*
> *you bring water from the sky and from*
> *deep in the Earth to cleanse and*
> *refresh us and keep us moist*
> *and living,*
> > *Forgive.*

*Mothers of Life,*
> *you give us days when the air is crisp and*
> *sweet-scented, and days when it is*
> *heavy with dew and the dampness*
> *of decay,*
> > *Forgive.*

Mothers of Life,
    you nurture us in the long bright days of
    summer and in the rich darkness
    of night and winter, you teach
    us the mysteries of the moon
    and stars,
        Forgive.

# CHAPTER 10

# The Hidden Mothers

The Mothers are hidden in the land. Perhaps it would be better to say that they are hiding in the land, preserving it, keeping it fertile, bringing forth life. They are invisible beings. But are they ever visible, or do they always remain just beyond the glance of the human eye?

Once in a small family-run restaurant in the West of Ireland, we asked the teenage waiter, a grandson of the owner, about the woman whose picture graced the Irish currency that the family had framed and hung on the wall to commemorate their first paying customers many decades ago. The bills were a former issue that today look quaint and old-fashioned, as did the mysterious woman on them.

"Ah," the young boy said, smiling assuredly, more to himself than to us. "She's the most beautiful woman in Ireland." He clearly used the present tense, yet the woman seemed to belong to a bygone era.

"Who is she?" we asked.

"Queen Maeve," he answered proudly, raising an eyebrow, hinting that perhaps he had personal acquaintance with her. "But it's not really Queen Maeve, you know," he continued. "Not exactly."

We braced ourselves for another typical Irish encounter with things-are-not-always-what-they-seem.

"It's actually Maud Gonne dressed up and posing as Queen Maeve," he explained as if it were important to know that, and then returned to the kitchen to fetch another tray of food. He seemed rather unconcerned as to whether we Americans knew who Maud Gonne is. Or was. Or who Maeve was. Or is.

Maud Gonne was a writer and Irish nationalist in the early twentieth century, a friend and inspiration to William Butler Yeats. So the former Irish currency had pictures of Maud Gonne posing as Queen Maeve! There was clearly more going on here than met the eye.

Maeve herself is wrapped in mystery. One of the earliest Irish goddesses, she has been historicized as a former queen of Connaught. As with so many figures in early Irish traditions, it is hard to separate myth and history. Ultimately, it probably doesn't matter to distinguish them. What matters is the abiding presence of these figures, at once ancient and modern, old and ever new, in time and beyond time.

Maeve is a goddess of sovereignty, fertility, and war. She is present when soldiers fight and die, when babies are born, when kings or presidents are inaugurated, when the land brings forth the summer's bounty and when it slumbers through the winter's dreaming. Her Irish name, Medb, is related to mead, so she is also the goddess of intoxication, or visions. As a queen in western Ireland, she was responsible for an epic war that was triggered by jealousy over her husband's cattle. She took up arms and fought alongside her warriors, and she brought about the death of the great champion Cuchulain through magic. She was indeed formidable. Is indeed formidable. She is one of the Mothers.

In Celtic traditions, Sovereignty is the goddess of the land, and any rightful king must be ritually married to her for his authority to be legitimate. The king, the state, the people, the land, the entire environment, and all aspects of prosperity depend upon her. Without her, to quote Yeats, things fall apart, the center does not hold. It is rather fitting that Maeve — or someone dressed up like her — should be on Irish money.

The euro has replaced national currency, but at the time of this writing, Maeve was still on all Irish money. As befits her otherworldly character, however, she is all but invisible on it. You must hold the note up to the light to see her, for her image — the most beautiful woman in Ireland — is encrypted in the paper as a watermark. Hidden in the fibers of the material, Maeve guards the Irish currency against counterfeiters. She continues to protect Ireland's prosperity.

It might be even more fitting that her face is not immediately visible to the naked eye, fitting that you have to hold the money up and let the light shine through. In a sense you have to look through the money to see the goddess of prosperity, just as you have to look *through* the physical elements to find the waters of Wisdom that flow from the Otherworld. Irish money teaches us that there is another reality behind the material world that money can buy.

All goddesses are like this. They are hidden. In the land. In the birthing of children. In the eyes of lovers. In the battle cries that scream across war-torn lands. In the final breath of the dying. In the first new shoots of grass in springtime. The Mothers are *always* present, even when they are as invisible as our own mothers were to us before we were born, when they were the warm, watery world in which we were conceived, grew, and took shape. When they were all that we knew.

As we live and walk upon the Earth today, we might recall that the land is the body of the Goddess, the Great Mother who will ever nurture us. If we let the light shine through our daily concerns, if we nurture that special way of seeing, that visionary approach to life, we can still glimpse the Mothers. And we understand in some strange and mysterious way that we still live within their sacred bodies. We have never really left. There may be nothing else we need to know.

# CHAPTER II

# Queen Maeve's Rules for Soul Making

Queen Maeve had three requirements for a husband. He was to be without fear, without jealousy, and without stinginess. These are appropriate requirements for soul making as well.

Speaking as the Goddess of Sovereignty, Maeve reminded kings that to be her consort they would have to be fearless warriors in defending the land. They would have to be tolerant of her many erotic relationships with other kings and chieftains whose authority and wisdom depended upon her good graces. Lastly, they would have to be generous, for in Celtic society the king was expected to be the most generous man in the realm or tribe. Maeve expected a lot from her husbands.

When it comes to soul making, fearlessness or courage is paramount, particularly when we consider that the soul extends beyond the body. If its expansiveness stretches to the ends of the earth, if the wind can carry our souls across the sky, we are raised to new levels of courage. There is a lot going on *out there* that we must not fear, even though it frightens us, disgusts us, repels us. Einstein said that the question every human being must answer before he or she dies is this: Is the universe a friendly place?

Among the Eskimo in the Arctic Circle there is a divine spirit named Sila who supports the Earth and all its life, both gentle and fierce, but whose voice is as "soft as a woman's." The Eskimo say that Sila is the "soul of the universe" and speaks "so fine and gentle that even children cannot become afraid. What Sila says is: "Be not afraid of the universe."[11] Soul making requires courage not to be afraid of the universe.

To be without jealousy is to be accepting and tolerant of what others have. If all things move through our souls, and help build our souls, then the good fortune of others is in some way our own. We should rejoice in the blessings that come to others for in some way those blessings are also ours. St. Paul put it this way: "All things are yours, and you are Christ's, and Christ is God's."[12]

Similarly, how can we be stingy if, by giving away our own goods and blessings, we really give them to others who are part of us? Sharing the good things of life with others increases the expansiveness of our souls. We are not diminished because what we give away is still part of the whole.

Maeve's demands are similar to the teachings of the ancient Druids. According to the classical writers, the Druids taught three important things: Honor the gods. Do no evil. Live courageously. These also are the stuff of soul making.

Live courageously even though circumstances frighten you. Push through fear, knowing that ultimately nothing can harm your soul.

Overcome jealousy and envy, and you short-circuit anger, hostility, vengeance, and other destructive feelings that can lead to harming someone else. Accept and understand the shortcomings of others, and you will do them no evil.

Honor the gods by honoring the divine spirit in all things. Give to others. Practice generosity. Occasionally even make physical offerings to the spirits in some way, as the tribal Celts did when they threw jewelry, tools, weapons, coins, and other expensive items into lakes and rivers to return material wealth to the Otherworld from which all good things come. Be hospitable and generous to strangers for they may be visitors from the Otherworld. Welcome the stranger at your door for it might be Christ.

No, it is not easy to be Maeve's consort. It is not easy to be a Druid. It is not always easy to take your soul seriously.

# CHAPTER 12

# RUSH HOUR

One afternoon while staying in Bantry Bay, I drove out the peninsula to enjoy the views of the ocean. On my return I was eager to get back for an evening dinner engagement, when a cluster of cows wandered out onto the narrow road in front of me. I honked gently at the cows, but they just turned their formidable rumps to me and began strolling slowly down the road ahead of me. Impatience began to surge up my American spine.

The road was terribly narrow, and hedgerows grew flush with the edge of the road so there was no shoulder on either side. I honked with more urgency, but the cows did not quicken their pace. It really didn't matter, because as I looked ahead I could see that even where the hedgerows ended, there were fences or hillsides or stone walls that did not allow any shoulder or widening of the roadbed for me to get around the cows. I eased up behind them at about three miles per hour, as close to them as possible without actually nudging them. They were not intimidated.

Surely, I thought, they will eventually find some way to move off the road and let me pass. But no way presented itself. This was going to be a long, long road.

Growing more impatient, I decided to try a little bluster. After all, I had a car. I stopped for a few moments to let them get a little farther ahead of me. Then, honking crazily, I drove up behind them as if to run them down. Two or three cows bringing up the rear of the herd parted slightly to let me through. The cows in front of them, however, were not impressed. They continued at their regular saunter, ignoring my threats. The ones that had let me pass closed ranks behind me, and I was then caught in the middle of the herd. My impatience was now peppered with claustrophobia. I had never driven so close to cows before. Still the road refused to widen.

We continued for another half mile or so, the cows not minding my presence in the least. I laid off the horn. As we moved slowly down the road, I had a feeling of defeat; in some way, I had lost. I felt very foreign to Irish roads, cows, the rural life. I felt strange. The kind of inept strangeness of a stranger. I started to wonder where my passport might be.

Then as our slow procession moved farther and farther down the road, a chilling thought occurred to me.

I'm rustling someone's cattle!

I looked around nervously, but saw no one. I began to worry about Irish laws regarding cattle stealing as I and the herd continued down the road to where I feared we might be miles from the owner's farm. How would I explain my behavior if I took them all the way into Bantry, where I would surely be apprehended?

When my panic was at its height, I looked in the rearview mirror and saw a truck leap out from nowhere and speed toward me, headlights flashing, horn blaring. It was the kind of truck that, in the United States, would undoubtedly have a gun rack in the cabin. I swallowed hard and slammed on the brakes (not that the three miles per hour needed brake slamming). The cows behind me picked up speed and passed me by. I prayed that whoever was pursuing me realized that the cows had only just then begun to run, and that I hadn't actually been running *them* down the road.

I pulled over to the left and let the truck pass. Then with considerable excitement, the truck blasted its way into the middle of the herd. Even the stalwart leaders parted to let it through. When the truck got a hundred feet or so in front of the cows, it stopped, and two men jumped out. They looked like father and son.

The men began flapping their arms violently and stalked menacingly toward the lead cows. They were talking to them. Fortunately, there was a narrow shoulder at that point, and the two men corralled the cows off to the side of the road. The younger man stayed with the cows. The older one started coming for me. He still walked at a menacing pace.

I wanted to be anywhere but Bantry Bay. I braced myself for the worst — the police, a fine, a night in the village jail.

But as the older farmer got closer, I could see that he was smiling sheepishly. He slowed down his walk, his hands clasped in front of his chest, almost as in prayer. When he got up to my car, he bowed his head, and removed his cap.

"Please forgive me and my cows," he began gently. "I hope they haven't caused you any grievances. They wander out sometimes like that. They have their own minds, you know. We didn't mean to frighten you, coming on so strong behind you, but sometimes it takes a little push to move them along."

I said yes, I know, and no, they hadn't, and I wasn't really frightened. I was trying to formulate a suitable apology for running his cows down the road, but he continued.

"I hope they haven't delayed you any." The concern in his voice and on his face was genuine.

I smiled. "No, they really haven't." I gave up on the apology.

"Well, be off now. And I hope you won't be upset about this little matter, or that it spoils your evening." He looked up at the sky. "It'll be a fine evening." He said that as if it were going to be a gift for me.

He replaced his cap and nodded farewell.

As I drove away, I wanted to reassure him that I was really not upset. After all, I was not going to spend the night in an Irish jail. But even more than that, how can you be upset with someone like him?

He was without fear, without anger, without stinginess.

He would have impressed even Queen Maeve.

# CHAPTER 13

# THE SHEEP AND THE GRAEL

There are two intriguing incidents in Celtic literature that, though both are minor episodes in two larger works, present a mystery that calls attention to one of the great spiritual insights found in many traditions.

The first concerns one of the fabulous islands that the Irish voyager Maelduin and his men encounter on their journey across the seas. The island is divided by a brass fence that separates two pastures of sheep. All the sheep on one side of the fence are black, while the sheep on the other side are white. There is a shepherd on the island who every now and then picks up a white sheep and places it across the fence with the black sheep, whereupon it turns black. Then he picks up a black sheep, places it among the white sheep, and it turns white.

Maelduin is intrigued as to whether this phenomenon is peculiar to sheep, or whether it is indigenous to the island itself. So he finds and peels two sticks, one white and one black. When he throws the white wand among the black sheep, the wand turns black. Conversely, the black wand turns white when tossed among the white sheep.

The Welsh hero Peredur has a similar adventure in his quest for the Grael. He wanders into a beautiful valley with healthy trees and a fine river dividing the glen in two. In a lush meadow on one side of the river is a flock of black sheep. A flock of white sheep grazes on the other side of the river. Every so often, a black sheep bleats, and a white sheep crosses the river to go to it. The white sheep then becomes black. When a white sheep bleats, a black sheep goes to it and turns white.

Peredur doesn't need to test this matter as Maelduin did. But Peredur sees something even more mysterious. Growing beside the river is a magnificent tree. Half of the tree is on fire, and the flames blaze up to the very top. But the other half is leafy and green and beautiful.

As in many Celtic tales, these incidents are not analyzed or explained. Nothing more comes of them. The hero accepts their strangeness and continues his quest. But what about us several centuries later? Can we bear to hear about such wonders and not ask the question: What does this strangeness mean?

The answer, of course, is up for grabs. But as we picture these two meadows of sheep, it is hard not to see in them another image that comes, not from Celtic lands, but from Asia. The black-and-white circle representing yin and yang. The circle is divided into white and black halves by a curving line in such a way that it does not create two distinctly separate hemispheres. The curved boundary allows part of the black area to intrude into the white half, and part of the white area to overlap onto the black side. To obscure the apparent duality even further, a small black spot lies within the white side, and a small white spot lies in the black half. The small spots might even be windows revealing the opposite color beneath the surface.

Much has been made of this simple image in terms of dualities and polarities. Since the symbol comes from China, a culture whose philosophies strongly argue against dualism, it can be viewed as a visual statement about how everything contains its opposite. Nothing is either black or white. Even though black and white exist, lurking in each color is the other. The yin-and-yang symbol is female and male, dark and bright, cold and hot, wet and dry, all the dualities that we can imagine. And hence from this union of all opposites, everything that is comes to be.

The meadows of the black-and-white sheep are a Celtic version of this same truth. Celtic mysticism, from Druidic times to the present, rejects dualism. In fact, all mystical traditions around the world reject it: the apparent dualities and opposites of ordinary reality are illusions. Everything contains its opposite; and the secret of life, the mysteries of being, are revealed only when we transcend, unite, or reconcile opposites.

Maelduin's voyage takes him to thirty-three islands, each with some bizarre situation that bends our notions of ordinary reality. Peredur's quest is for the Grael, the vessel of wisdom and grace that fades in and out of our world and that mysterious Otherworld. Like Maelduin's miraculous islands, the Grael is both in and not in ordinary reality. We must become seekers, voyagers, journeyers into that other reality where white becomes black and vice versa, where good and evil do not exist, where the Great Split of Me and Not-Me is reconciled.

The wonder voyages are considered to be a "Celtic book of the dead" intended to teach the living about death. In the Grael stories, only Galahad looks directly into the sacred vessel, and then dies, suggesting that the ultimate realization of the Grael mysteries will have to wait until our Earthly lives are over. There is much in these tales that suggests we will only know the full mystery after we die. But that does not discourage us from seeking it now.

The Buddhists say, "The Buddha Way is unattainable. I vow to attain it." Following their example, we might say, "The Grael is unknowable. I vow to know it. The Grael is unfindable. I vow to find it."

In the meantime we stumble through life, tripping over the dualities and opposites that build our souls. But once those experiences merge in the great cauldron of the soul, they lose their distinctive otherness. We lose *our* distinctive otherness. We grow in wisdom and grace, learning that the Great Split is illusion. We discover that the black-and-white sheep only appear so in certain meadows, and that one miraculous tree can be both firewood, burning intensely as on a cold winter night, and greenwood, bursting joyously with the leaves of summer.

# CHAPTER 14

# The Three Harpers

There is an old Irish legend about Uaithne (pronounced "oo-uh-nyeh"), who was the official harper for the Irish god known as the Dagda. When Uaithne's wife, Boann (for whom the Boyne River is named) gave birth, he accompanied her with the Music of Weeping to participate with her in a painful delivery. When the baby boy was born, they named him Goltrai, which means "sad song." Then a second baby arrived! This time the delivery was so pleasant that Boann smiled and laughed, so Uaithne played the Music of Laughter to share in her joy. The second boy was named Gentrai, which means "happy song." Then a third boy was born, and Boann fell asleep during the delivery, so tired and at peace was she. Uaithne played a lullaby to accompany her, and they named the third baby Suantrai, which means "lullaby."

Needless to say, the three boys grew up to become harpers, each specializing in his particular type of music.

But more remarkable, these three Gods of the Harp became the model for every Irish harper after them. For to become a professional harper, one was expected to play these three strains of music in order to move listeners from sorrow to joy to sleep. While in a peaceful sleep, drowsed by the haunting strings of the harp, their ills were cured, their worries resolved, and they woke refreshed and healed. For harpers and poets (who often accompanied themselves on harps) were singers of healing songs. They were healers.

Another version of the old tale is that it was the Dagda's harp itself that was named Uaithne, and the music that the god played on this harp kept the seasons in proper order. Uaithne means "verdant," "greenness," the green of nature, the color of fertile land, the juice that brings seasons of growth and plenty. When the gods of chaos and destruction, the Fomorians, stole Uaithne, they discovered that they could not play it. Or rather, it would not allow itself to be played, for the music of growth, fertility, and health is alien to the gods of destruction. When the Dagda rescued his harp, he called to it with these words: "Come, summer; Come, winter; Come, voice of harp, voice of flute, voice of pipe."

So we learn that the healing music of the gods is also the music that will heal the Earth and keep it fertile and life supporting. In medieval times, philosophers spoke of the "music of the spheres," that divine harmony which permeates the universe and maintains the many individual harmonies and balances of a healthy cosmos. We might say that the medievalists had a musical version of the Navajo idea of "walk in beauty." We might imagine them asking people to "dance in beauty" — which means to be in step, in balance with the divine harmonies that maintain cosmic health.

There are many Irish tales of harpers playing the three strains of music to heal someone. I once wondered why there were not simply two: sorrow and joy. After all, isn't the idea of healing to move a person out of sorrow, pain, and suffering and into joy, happiness, and well-being? You would think so. But one day as I was (metaphorically) wandering around in the meadow of the black-and-white sheep, I remembered that that kind of duality is not the answer. Everything contains its opposite. While a period of joy and happiness might be fine for awhile, surely sorrow and suffering will return. "Come, summer; come, winter." Both are necessary.

Perhaps the music of sleep is required to produce the tranquil state *beyond* joy and sorrow, a preview of the ultimate consciousness in which all dualities are reconciled, a brief glimpse of that dreamland where the tension between opposites is transcended. Perhaps this is similar to what Buddhists call satori, or the nirvana of Hinduism, or the beatific vision of God in Christianity. Celtic harpers used the divine music to heal Earthly suffering, not just with a return to joy but to a state of peace and tranquillity, a fertile void where the tension of opposites ceases, and we know, or remember, the blessed state of ecstasy to which we will someday return. This Earthly peace is, of course, a prelude to death.

Try this the next time you want to pray for someone who is in pain or sick or worried, or just suffering through some troublesome period in life. Sit down, use a small rattle or drum if you have one, and visualize the face of the person in pain. Then softly begin to hum, letting the hum become a sound, a word, an expression of sorrow that allows you to participate with that person in his or her suffering. Sing or chant this for awhile, then let it turn into a happier melody of words or sounds, and see that person's face begin to smile, laugh, and rejoice. Share in these happier feelings while you continue to sing. Then watch the person fall peacefully asleep, and allow your singing to become restful, like a lullaby. Sing your friend into that state of perfect bliss where no opposites exist, where we can be one with our own souls, with the universe, with God.

When you have finished singing, ask yourself, "What is it I have just done? And why do *I* feel so good?"

# CHAPTER 15

# Most This
# Amazing Day

The reason you felt so good after singing a song of healing for another person is that you immersed yourself in the *power of the word.* Even if you simply hummed, or merely sang simple vocables, your voice, your breath, and your unique spirit have the power to heal. Your enspirited voice can heal *you* as well as others.

A voice has tremendous and dangerous power. Words of encouragement can truly encourage; curse words can cause great harm; words of helpful criticism help; words that are meant to demean can destroy another's spirit. St. John tells us that "In the beginning was the Word," and It was God, and through It all things were made.[13]

Our voices, although they are only faint echoes of the Divine Voice, continue to make, unmake, and remake.

We live in a culture so saturated with verbiage that we become oblivious to the power of the word. We take words for granted; we see and hear too many of them in the course of a day. They become nuisances. Or we become so addicted to words that to be alone and silent drives us crazy. Yet all men and women of every age and culture who sought the sacred in their lives, the saints and mystics, recognized the need for silence and solitude. They longed for periods of retreat and withdrawal from the world in which they could follow the divine directive in the Old Testament, "Be still, and know that I am God."[14]

Sitting quietly and singing the three songs of healing for someone is like entering a sacred space where you can use your voice differently from the usual chatter of the day. You allow your spirit and its good wishes, blessings, and love for someone suffering to emerge from between your lips empowered by the breath of life. That spirit flies forth with healing and travels far beyond the actual reach of your voice. It spans the distance between you and the one in pain, where spirit speaks to spirit, and something within the person responds, feels better, finds hope, is healed, is created.

The power of the word came home to me on a trip to Donegal, that wild, rugged, sparsely populated northwestern corner of Ireland. I had spent four days visiting a friend named Miriam and her young daughter, and on my last evening there when we went to the pub, we discovered that one of the two small rooms that comprised the pub had been reserved for a private party. But in the spirit of hospitality typical of Celtic gatherings, you didn't have to be in the "in-group" to be invited.

Miriam and I would never have qualified for the in-group anyway. It was a class of disabled teenagers who had spent their spring camping trip in Donegal and were celebrating their last night before returning to Belfast. They and their teachers were enjoying the "crack" (*craic* in Gaelic means "fun") of recounting their adventures of the week. The small room was literally crackling with laughter and conviviality. Teachers raising glasses of Guinness, students swigging Cokes. As we entered, someone asked our names and invited us to sit down.

At some point, the head teacher, a young, hip fellow from Denmark with an explosion of black, shaggy hair, asked if any of the kids wanted to recite a poem or sing a song. I was totally flabbergasted by the response. Everyone wanted to! Including the teachers. And they did. Adolescents who displayed various types of physical or developmental disabilities rose from their chairs, one at a time, to recite a poem or sing a song, often lengthy and complicated ones that must have required hours of memorization. Traditional Irish folksongs, a Gerard Manley Hopkins poem, a song of lost love from a girl who seemed excruciatingly shy, a Shakespeare sonnet. A boy with incredibly thick glasses and a twitching, muscular disorder had to be told by a solicitous teacher that there was not time for him to recite the entirety of *A Midsummer Night's Dream.* (Another teacher sitting nearby whispered to me, "He can do it. He has a photographic memory.") To each performer, the group offered spontaneous and heartfelt applause, compliments, and good-natured teasing.

Miriam and her daughter had left early, and I huddled deeply into the corner, enjoying the party, pretending to be invisible. But it was just a matter of time before the head teacher pointed to me, wrapped around my pint of Guinness, and said, "Come on, Tom, you can't hide in a corner. You surely have a poem for us."

Although he was young enough to be my son, I suddenly felt like a high school student again, called upon by the teacher to stand up and answer a question I wasn't at all ready for. He was right: I couldn't hide; everyone looked my way, and so I stood up. I mentally riffed through my meager repertoire, selected an e. e. cummings poem that I thought I knew, and began to recite it.

> *i thank You God for most this amazing  day: for*
> *the leaping greenly spirits of trees and a blue*
> *true dream of sky; and for everything which is*
> *natural which is infinite which is yes* . . . [15]

Although I had not recited that poem in years, I managed to plow my way through it, to the last beautiful lines: "now the ears of my ears awake and / now the eyes of my eyes are opened." I sat down to a great round of applause that seemed all out of proportion to the quality of the performance. I went back to my Guinness.

I hate karaoke, but somehow this felt good. I felt good. Nevertheless, I was glad it was over. I could enjoy the rest of the evening. I was off the hook. Or so I thought.

During a break, the local folksinger who had been hired for the party asked me where I was from originally, and I told her St. Louis. She confided that she had always wanted to hear the blues played in a Mississippi River town. I shared with her some memories of the music I had heard during the years I lived in St. Louis and Memphis. Then she asked me if I could sing "Ol' Man River." A lump dropped in my stomach.

Unfortunately, I can.

Immediately she stood up, clapped her hands for attention, asked for silence, and announced before I could refuse that "Tom's going to sing a famous song from his homeland for us." And so I did. Sort of. It seemed not to matter to them that I was not African-American with a deep baritone voice backed by powerful lungs who could actually sing on key. I wasn't any of that. But as my cracking (or was it craicing?) voice slid around on the lyric "he don't plant cotton," I realized that it didn't matter to them that I am not a professional, or even polished, singer of songs.

Cotton! The kids' eyes lit up. I had lived on the Mississippi, I had seen cotton, I knew about "taters," as they did. I was now one of the party, and really that was all that mattered. I didn't have to be good. I had a song, and it's the song that contains the magic.

As I walked the drizzly road back to the bed-and-breakfast where I was staying, I floated along ecstatically remembering the evening's voices running through my head. The voice of the boy with Tourette's syndrome, the girl with the disfigured leg, the painfully shy girl who stuttered except when she recited poetry, the "slow" boy who seemed to elicit more attention and praise from his comrades than any other. Each had uttered joyous words of healing.

How remarkable the evening had been, comprised of nothing but average voices, shy and hesitant, proud yet unselfconscious, the voices of Ireland's youth. Each young man and woman was imbibed with the Celtic spirit that knows how important it is to "have a poem" for someone.

I thank you, God, for most that amazing night . . . "now the ears of my ears awake and / now the eyes of my eyes are opened."

# CHAPTER 16

# The Winds of Fate

I sometimes think about those teenagers from Belfast with their songs, poems, teachers, dreams, friends, and their disabilities. And I wonder what winds blew at their births.

An Irish poem called "The Winds of Fate" tells how the wind blesses each child when it is born. A child who is born when the north wind blows will wound, and be wounded. The child who is born with the east wind blowing will never know want. If the south wind blows, the child will have music and entertainment in his or her life. When the west wind blows, the child will be given food, shelter, and clothing in life, but nothing more. A child who is born when no wind blows will be a fool.

These qualities assigned to the four directions (or airts, as they're called in Gaelic) go far deeper into the Celtic past than this more recent poem about the wind. An ancient myth confirms that these same qualities assigned to the four directions have been part of the Irish heritage for centuries.

In a time outside of time, a mysterious visitor appeared before the assembled tribes of Ireland and announced that he would teach the seven wisest people from each of the five provinces of Ireland stories appropriate to the indigenous qualities of those provinces. He then asked the people what was in each of the Irish provinces. A wise seer replied that in the north was battle, in the east was prosperity, in the south was music, and in the west was vision. The center was kingship, sovereignty, responsibility.

And hearing this, the mysterious visitor from the Otherworld told the first stories in Ireland to the first storytellers. They were stories about battle; work and home life; music, entertainment, and creativity; vision and destiny; and the responsibility to hold the center. And those stories, in some form or other, are still told to this very day.

Surely all the winds were blowing fine and strong when these remarkable adolescents were born. The north wind brought each of them a personal battle, a woundedness in mind or body, but it also bestowed the courage of spirit to struggle and win victories despite those wounds. The east wind brought them to the Belfast Waldorf school, a home where they can live and prosper as they pursue their studies and seek a vision for their lives. Not all disabled teenagers are so lucky. Their last night in the pub was proof enough that the south wind blew: there was a song or a poem in each of them. And it is hard not to believe that the west wind sent those dedicated, inspiring teachers who are giving them the knowledge and courage to understand their visions — to go beyond food, shelter, and clothing, as the poem states, and discover the meaning of their lives.

Carved on the massive upright of a ninth-century stone cross at the monastery of Clonmacnoise are scenes that echo these same directional qualities. The north face of the cross depicts a man fighting a dragon; the east face shows St. Peter welcoming the faithful to the eternal prosperity of Heaven on Judgment Day; the south side depicts a man, possibly David, with his harp; and the west side shows the purpose of Jesus' life: his betrayal, crucifixion, and resurrection — the destiny for which he was born.

I have come to believe that this simple pattern of the four airts, along with their vital center, contains all the events of our lives, and the necessary virtues to meet life's challenges successfully. The four airts are a kind of Irish "medicine wheel."

In the north are all our battles, conflicts, struggles, and foes. Here we defend what we believe in, fight against injustice, and find the courage to stand up and be counted, and the courage to make peace.

In the east is the prosperity that comes from hard

work and the life we build with those we love. Here are jobs, careers, homes, families, neighborhoods. In the east is also the deep well of generosity with which we share with others the good things that life bestows on us.

The south nurtures all our creativity and entertainment, the arts and crafts that enrich our lives, the ways we play and have fun, the things we do to make others laugh. In the south we hear the songs of our hearts, the deepest music in our souls, and we find the inspiration and self-confidence to sing those songs and dance to that music.

And in the west is the knowledge of who we are, where we come from, why we are here, and where we are going. We create a vision for ourselves and discover the meaning of our lives. In the west we find the faith and steadfastness to never give up, even in the darkest nights of our souls when we are tempted to doubt that life has meaning.

The winds of fate blow at our births, and they continue to blow all our life long. They are ever shifting. As the Gospels remind us, the wind blows where it wants to, no one knows where it comes from, and no one knows where it goes.

CHAPTER 17

# †aki∏g Charge of †he Ce∏ter

In the center of the Irish medicine wheel is Sovereignty. In the old myth of the first stories, the seer tells the visitor from the Otherworld that the center is kingship. Early Celtic political theory affirmed that the king has authority only because he is ritually married to the Goddess of Sovereignty, who is also the Goddess of the Land, the Mother of Life. Our earlier prayer asking the Mothers of Life for forgiveness is a way to place ourselves in the position of the king by acknowledging that we often fail in our lives because, like a wayward ruler or chieftain, we forget our responsibilities to Sovereignty.

What or who is Sovereignty?

In a number of legends and folktales several brothers are confronted by a loathsome, foul-smelling hag who seeks shelter on a miserable night. The older brothers tell her, in effect, to get lost. But the youngest invites her to share his bed by the fire. In some tales he kisses her; in others he makes love to her. In the morning the woman at his side is young and beautiful. He asks who she is, and she replies, "Sovereignty." She disappears, but sees to it that he, the youngest brother, becomes the next chieftain or king.

The king holds the central place in the wheel of life; he is the hub in the circle of battle, prosperity, music, and vision. When he rules from a deep-seated understanding of the Truth of his position, his realm flourishes, whole, healthy, and life affirming. The King's Truth is responsible for almost every aspect of Celtic society, and that Truth, his authority, comes from the divine feminine, the Goddess Sovereignty who resides in the land.

A high king in the first century A.D. was instructed by his Druid adviser about the critical importance of the King's Truth:

*By the King's Truth great clans are ruled,*
*By the King's Truth great death is warded off,*
*By the King's Truth great battles are driven off*
    *into the enemy's country,*
*By the King's Truth every right prevails,*
*By the King's Truth every vessel is full,*
*By the King's Truth fine weather comes in each*
    *fitting season: winter fine and frosty, spring*

*dry and windy, summer warm with showers*
*of rain, autumn heavy with dew and fruitful,*
*By the King's Truth the land is fruitful and*
*every child born is worthy,*
*By the King's Truth there is abundance of tall*
*corn.*

*Let him magnify the Truth, it will magnify him,*
*Let him strengthen the Truth, it will strengthen*
*him,*
*Let him guard the Truth, it will guard him,*
*Let him exalt the Truth, it will exalt him.*[16]

For years I have searched Celtic traditions for a concept similar to the Navajo *horzo,* or "Beauty," the kind of beauty that comes from being in harmony with the universe, in step with the natural laws, and aligned with the "fitness of things." I've come to the conclusion that the closest Celtic term is *fírinne,* which is usually translated as "Truth." Truth with a capital *T.* Not the truth that refers simply to whether someone is lying or deceiving another, not the truth dictated by religious institutions or schools of philosophy, not the truth that reflects the current scientific understandings. None of these is deep enough or eternal enough. Truth, like the Navajo's Beauty, is a relationship with life, a relationship known deep in the soul that balances our personal lives with the Great Life Itself.

A Scottish morning prayer from the nineteenth century says, "I thank you, Dearest God, that I have risen again today to the rising of this Great Life Itself. As the morning mist scatters from the crests of the hills, may every ill haze clear from my soul."[17]

This prayer poignantly expresses the idea of Truth as relationship — the Truth that we learn from living in harmony with the Great Life Itself, when we see that what occurs in nature has reflections in the soul. This is the Truth we find in nature, in the cosmos, in the well-ordered human community that balances the needs and wants of all its members with the environment. Tribe and Land — in the harmonious living and working of these two great entities we discover Truth.

The word *sovereignty* is a strange term. We don't use it every day, and it reeks of monarchical forms of government or dreary courses in political science. And yet, on the personal level each of us must come to terms with it. Perhaps better words are *accountability* and *responsibility*. It is the ruler, man or woman, sitting in the center who has responsibility for the whole realm, precisely because he or she is actively engaged in the give-and-take of life on the periphery. The ruler is accountable for the four divisions of the sacred wheel of life. The one who sits in the place of the King should be the foremost and bravest warrior, the most generous host, outshining all others in hospitality, the most committed patron of the arts and entertainment. And no ruler in Celtic society was without an official Druid, a personal adviser who spoke with the voice of reason, vision, wisdom, and spiritual knowledge.

In the wheel of our own lives, we are the rulers, we

hold the scepter of responsibility for ourselves, for the tribe of our family and associates, and for our environment. We are accountable. This doesn't mean that we can control our lives or all the people and situations that make up our lives. Sovereignty is not about being in control. It is about taking charge.

Prisoners, the dying, children, the homeless, refugees, the unemployable, and many others are not in control of their lives. But they can take charge of their lives. They can decide how they will respond to what life offers them. They can vow that their *response* to the challenges of life will be truly their own.

The morning prayer that recognizes a direct relationship between the mist on the hills and the haze in our souls could be our model prayer for Sovereignty. To live each day with gratitude that our humble lives are part of the Great Life Itself, and with the understanding that what happens in nature and the world around us reflects the movements in our souls. When we are so balanced with nature, ourselves, and the many spokes on the Wheel of Life Itself, then we can say with the Navajo that we "walk in Beauty" and with the Celtic ruler that we "walk in Truth."

# CHAPTER 18

# WALK IN TRUTH

To walk in Truth has challenging and dangerous implications for daily life. It is not easy to live in right relationship with Truth.

St. Patrick asked one of Finn MacCool's men (who returned from the Otherworld years after his death) what sustained the warriors of the Fianna during those years before Christianity. The old saint seemed unable to imagine that anyone could lead a meaningful and spiritually vigorous life without knowledge of the Gospels. The former warrior-hunter answered, "The Truth in our hearts, the Strength in our arms, and the Promise on our lips." In a nutshell he summarized the old Celtic moral code: to live from the deep inner knowledge of the heart and soul, to manifest it by physical action, and to be true to one's word.

Truth with a capital *T* includes telling the truth. We saw earlier that the high king Cormac was led into the otherworldly realm called the Land of Truth to discover the Pool of Wisdom with its hazelnuts, salmon, and the five running streams of water that bring divine wisdom through our five senses. During his sojourn, he was also given the Cup of Truth to bring back into our world.

The Cup of Truth was a magical vessel that cracked and fell apart when a lie was spoken across it. Conversely, when the truth was spoken, it restored itself to wholeness. As king, Cormac used the Cup of Truth to render wise judgments in disputes among his people. It would be interesting to see what would happen with such a cup today. Our culture is based on so many official and unofficial falsehoods, misleading propositions, and downright lies. If they were exposed, society itself might crack apart, just as living a lie can crack the integrity of an individual soul.

Thomas the Rhymer was taken by the Elf Queen to be her lover for seven years. When he left Elf Land, she gave him the ability to foresee future events and, after returning to our world, his reputation as a great seer spread throughout Scotland. But he was also blessed or cursed (depending on how you view it) with the inability to tell a lie, a trait that sometimes proved rather embarrassing when he was forced to speak the truth in situations that required social or political reticence concerning the facts. After all, only a naive, innocent child can actually say out loud that the emperor has no clothes!

It is odd that human society requires the suppression of truth in certain circumstances and that we believe that this is how it should be. Is it because a constant awareness of dark truths and Truth Itself is too intense for everyday life? We may be able to live with only small doses of Life Itself and Truth Itself, judging by what the great mystics have told us about the intensity of divine revelation. The most profound mystical experiences can be shattering to the human psyche. The divine brightness radiating from them is too much for the ordinary human life. Does this also apply to Truth Itself, and to the social truths we overlook day after day?

We learn to live with artificiality and social requirements that contradict the deeper Truth in our souls. Perhaps the source of so much human discontent is that we recognize and eventually tolerate deception, social posing, misleading statements, and official and unofficial lies from public leaders and the media. We learn to tolerate what the Truth in our hearts tells us is intolerable. We become bedfellows with what we know is wrong, and call it right. We are in danger of fulfilling Henry David Thoreau's great fear: to come to the end of our lives and discover that what we have lived is not Life.

Death, then, becomes a great and welcome release. We leave this world of falsehoods and agreed-upon deceptions for that state of consciousness where we can be flooded with Truth. Death escorts us into the blessed realms where we will have the capacity for Truth, Enlightenment, the Beatific Vision, unfiltered, undisguised, and uninterrupted by the misconceptions of the human world. We no longer need to see as "through a glass, darkly." When a person dies in Ireland, the expression of sympathy is to say, "Ah, he (or she) is in the place of Truth now."

The dead have left this world — this confusing human environment created partly from the ever-shifting values and obligations of history, current fashion, and chance into which each of us is born. When the world knocks our souls off center and frightens us, we may try to save ourselves by pulling our souls ever tighter around our lives in the mistaken belief that to cut ourselves off from the world will preserve our connection to Life Itself. But such withdrawal is ultimately self-defeating because the soul cannot hide in the body or its shadow. The soul is expansive and wants to reach outward, even through fear, so that it will grow in wisdom and truth. But to reach out to the world is not the same as embracing it. We must be in the world but not of it. At times, we must oppose it.

We might adopt Boudica's battle cry when she rallied her armies against the Romans, fighting for the right of Celtic people to be both in charge and in control of their own lives. "The Truth against the World!" she cried. Sadly, her rebellion failed, she was killed, and Rome solidified its control over Britain. Nevertheless, she and her warriors fought with Truth, Strength, and Promise.

The Truth in our hearts, the Strength in our arms, the Promise on our lips. And if we break that Promise, if we do not live true to our word, "May the sky fall upon us, may the sea rise up and drown us, and may the earth crack open and swallow us." This old Celtic warrior oath is not just a plea for the elements to punish us if we break our promises. It is an affirmation that the cosmos itself is the Cup of Truth. Our lies, our falsehoods, our broken promises can pull the sky and sea and earth apart and shatter them.

# CHAPTER 19

# HOME RUNS
# IN A NEMETON

One autumn I wandered down a trail at a Methodist camp in central New York State where a group of us hold our shamanic practitioners' yearly reunion. The trail marker at a fork in the path indicated the ball field was to the left, and I took the left fork. As I hiked along, I was impressed that the ball field was so isolated from the lake, main buildings, cabins, dining hall, and other facilities. Some summer camps seem to be nothing but ball fields. What first catches your eye as you drive through the rustic gate welcoming you to this kind of camp is the chain-link fencing behind home plate, the dusty infield with worn bases, the weathered spectator stands, and sometimes way down in the farthest outfield (as strange as it seems) a basketball court. All of this makes some kind of sense, I suppose, except that it jars my personal sense of why we go to summer camp in the first place. Not to play softball or basketball, not to cheer temporary teams of homesick children, not to do what millions of kids are doing in every schoolyard, city park, and urban playground all year round.

We go to camp to find trees.

As I continued my hike, I began to suspect that I had taken a wrong turn, assuming that the ball field surely couldn't be so remote from the center of camp. But no, I was on the right trail, and suddenly the forest parted, and I stepped out into a large grassy, tree-rimmed clearing that would have sent a Druid's heart into spasms of ecstasy. Here was a glorious, open, almost perfectly circular, sun-drenched, autumn-leafed, breezy New York State nemeton.

A nemeton! The antique Roman-Celtic word for one of the holiest places in Celtic spirituality. In the old Gallic language, *nemeton* meant "sacred clearing." The Latin word *nemus* meant "sacred woods." In Greek *tenemos* was land dedicated to a deity. In Welsh and Breton the root word *nem* means "heaven." In Old Irish *nemed* meant "sanctuary," and *fidnemed*, a forest shrine or sacred grove. Not having been much of a ballplayer in my life, I was surprised to step out into a ball field and feel a certain hallowed rush come over me.

But it was not just a ball field. It was a nemeton.

In fact, much to my amazement, I saw no clear indications of home plate, bases, a pitcher's mound, foul lines, or any other common features of a standard playing field. I heard no echoes in this clearing that shouted, "Play ball!" "Safe!" "You're out!" Everything was grassy and hushed in what I imagine was the same quiet, woodland sanctity that impressed my Celtic ancestors when they cleared their own nemetons, or found them, deep in the ancient forests of old Europe.

Off to one side in the clearing I found a circular stone fire pit with the remains of cold, charred logs, the vestiges of a recent bonfire perhaps from some late-summer night. Did this ball field also serve some nonathletic purpose? I felt like an archaeologist stumbling upon some ancient site whose mysteries now elude us. Did those campers sing camp songs like "Cowboy Lullaby" or "Angels Watching Over Me"? Maybe it was a closing campfire, and each boy and girl tossed in a twig and dedicated it to someone special and made a solemn promise of how they would change their lives when they got back home.

I reverently walked to the center of the clearing, basking in the warm autumn sunlight. I sensed the numinous all around me. I was alone, but not alone. All sacred circles put you "betwixt and between," they make you feel alone but vulnerable to the eyes that watch. From where? Deep in the trees. From the sky above. From earlier ages. Stepping into any circle's center — whether of trees or standing stones — is to make yourself at once vulnerable to the expansiveness of the universe and, at the same time, to experience the comfort of the encompassing, embracing wholeness that surrounds you. It turns you around. It stretches your soul. You feel like you are neither here nor there. It can make you dizzy.

The sacred has always had the connotation of terror. Jewish-Christian texts speak of the "fear of the Lord." Moses trembled before the burning bush. Mystics are often terrified by the divine power they merely glimpse in its brilliant glory. Too much of the numinous, and we go berserk. We have to look upon this power "through a glass, darkly," or wear expensive sunglasses.

The Roman writer Lucan described, in the first century A.D., the Druidic sanctuaries as dark, gloomy, and sinister; uninhabited by decent Roman deities; hostile to birds and wild animals; windless; resounding with fearsome tremors from the horrible caves nearby; and infested with dragons roaming through the trees. People, he wrote, even priests themselves, feared to enter such frightening places.

Lucan was not impressed with Celtic spirituality. Viewing non-Roman customs through the eyes of an outsider, he may have misinterpreted the Druids' reluctance to enter the wooded sanctuaries except on certain prescribed occasions and in a certain awe-inspired manner. He may have interpreted this formalized respect as fear of what his Roman sensibilities considered barbaric and sadistic deities. Or maybe it wasn't his fault at all. Maybe something more "sinister" was afoot, something like a crafty Druid purposely telling gullible outsiders like Lucan that the nemetons were indeed dangerous and unfit for human beings. Maybe this Druid exaggerated the horrors with great bardic flourish precisely to scare away the likes of Lucan and keep them out of the sacred nemetons. I would have.

A nemeton is a wonderful betwixt-and-between place, a place where, when you step out from the darkness beneath the trees, the glorious expanse of sky greets you almost joyously and upliftingly, showering you with daylight and fresh air. Your spirits rise. Here is a marriage point of heaven and earth. Here is a place between the worlds of ordinary physical reality and the non-ordinary spiritual reality of our prayers and dreams. A place that is neither here nor there, where you can feel the closeness of heaven, the realms of faery, ancestral presences, the mysterious Otherworld, and maybe last summer's children.

Here in the sacred circle of trees, in the holy clearing we are not sure where we are. Perhaps (to give Lucan some credit, but not too much) not knowing where you are can indeed be frightening, if it is not liberating. Ask yourself, "When I step out of the forest and into the clearing, am I still in the forest?"

I like to think that even the logical, imperial, straight-road-building, engineering — yes, even baseball-playing — mind of a Roman would have to succumb to the classic Celtic answer to that question.

Are you still in the forest?

Well, you are and you aren't.

# CHAPTER 20

# CIRCLES OF MYSTERY

hen Scottish and Irish people bank their fires down at night before going to bed, they traditionally say a prayer similar to this one:

*I smoor this night my fire,*
*God's compassing be to myself and the fire,*
*God's compassing to myself and to all,*
*God's compassing to myself and the hearth,*
*God's compassing to myself and the floor,*
*And upon each herd and flock,*
*And upon the household all.*[18]

Another old Celtic prayer for protection reads:

*The arm of Mary Mother be yours,*
*The arm of Brigid of the flocks be yours,*
*The arm of Michael victorious be yours . . .* [19]

The prayer then repeats this type of blessing, calling on the arms of the Apostles John, Paul, and Peter. Finally the arms of the Trinity Itself are invoked:

*The arm of the God of life be yours,*
*The arm of Christ the loving be yours,*
*The arm of the Spirit Holy be yours,*
*To shield you and surround you.*

A third type of "encompassing" prayer to the Three of Power goes:

*The Three Who are over me,*
*The Three Who are below me,*
*The Three Who are above me here,*
*The Three Who are above me yonder,*
*The Three Who are in the Earth,*
*The Three Who are in the air,*
*The Three Who are in the heavens,*
*The Three Who are in the great pouring sea.*[20]

In some prayers, Jesus or God or the Trinity are referred to as the "encirclers." In other prayers the saints and holy ones are asked to protect us by means of their "shields" or their "mantles."

We see in these prayers and invocations a deep

faith that protection in daily life comes from being surrounded by holy power, divine power. Calling on the
Divine Spirit who is in the earth, air, heavens, and sea
reminds us of the Gaelic word *dúile* — the elements —
and the power of the Dúileamh in the many *dúile* of
creation. The Creator is inseparable from creation, and
so divine power and protection are always encompassing us for the simple reason that we are always encom-
passed by creation.

These prayers are similar to the Navajo prayer that
states that there is Beauty "before me, behind me,
above me, beneath me," wherever I walk. A Celtic version of this goes:

> *God before me, God behind me,*
> *God above me, God below me,*
> *I on the path of God,*
> *God on my track, too.*[21]

What we are seeing here is an adaptation of the
nemeton, the sacred clearing, where, if we are suffi-
ciently sensitive to the spirit, we instinctively recognize
the numinous all around us. We feel the eye or arm of
God. These are prayers to ask that the encompassing,
surrounding power that we experience in a circle of
wholeness, even though that circle consist only of trees
deep in the forest, accompany us throughout the day
and night. But lest this all sound too cozy, we are also
face-to-face with the "terror" of the nemeton.

Standing in the open center stimulates feelings of

vulnerability, for the circle is also a lure, calling to something deep in our souls to expand and to fill that space. Such a call can be terrifying, and we instinctively seek protection, for most of us have not yet realized the expansiveness of the soul that surrounds the body. We have not yet found or developed the faith to believe and trust in the basic goodness of the universe around us. I find it naturally intimidating to hear a call to fill the entire universe. Nevertheless, I was created to do just that if I believe that the mystics' description of being one with and filled with All That Is applies to me too.

It seems we have a choice. To believe that our souls are hidden inside our bodies where, we hope, they will be protected until we die and they are whisked away to heavenly safety. Or to believe that our bodies, minds, egos, and personalities are temporarily living within the soul, and that this soul exists to fill the entire universe. The first alternative usually implies that God is transcendent, somewhere in the heavenly realms, and we are in exile here on Earth, waiting to be released from this valley of tears. The second implies that God is right here, in the wind, sea, stars, flowers, storms — and the arm of God is around us. God walks in our footprints even as we step into God's. We are already with God, and God is with us. Death, then, releases us from the Great Illusion that we are separate from the One Who Is and All That Is.

These old prayers are more in the nature of reminders than petitions. They often don't so much ask for divine assistance as acknowledge that it already accompanies us. We merely need to be reminded of it.

There is an old folk method for casting this power and protection around oneself. It is called the *caim,* a Gaelic word that means "loop," "bend," "crookedness," or "distortion." The word is also used in the expression "to refract a ray of light." To make the *caim,* you extend your right arm outward in front of you, with your index finger pointing, and turn sunwise, or clockwise, while reciting a prayer similar to the ones above. In effect, you are ritually drawing, with your finger, the circle of protection around yourself. If harm comes your way, this circle of power refracts it away from you.

Some people, of course, claim that such a practice is superstitious. And indeed it is! That's why it's so wonderful and powerful to do it! *Superstition* means to "stand above," and that is precisely what a ritual re-minder, like the *caim,* is: a call to stand above your present situation and view it from on high, to overcome myopic, low-level vision, and to see what is really going on around you.

Looking down at yourself from above, what do you see? Circles inside circles inside circles of divine mys-tery! Or to put it more simply, as the old prayers do, you see the arms of God around you.

# CHAPTER 21

# The Big Bang of Divine Life

According to an old European mystery tradition that goes back to Plato, all created things share in the divine life of the Creator. In fact, it was the Creator's desire to share and expand that divine life that resulted in creation. In a sense, by creating the planets, stars, elements, animals, human beings, all wildlife, and all the spiritual entities that exist, the Creator multiplied the forms, shapes, and possibilities for divine life to manifest and experience itself.

Another way to put it is that divine life is such a good thing that even the Creator yearns for it, yearns to have it more abundantly, and so allows it to spill over and flow out and reshape itself in the varied forms of physical life that make up our universe. And the result is that the Creator finds all things not only good but also lovable.

God yearns for the goodness in us, in nature, and in all things, and loves it.

One of the classical mystery writers on this subject was a man (most likely) whose identity eludes us since he wrote under the pen name of Dionysius, and who was supposedly a disciple of St. Paul. Scholars know, however, that the actual writer lived several centuries later, judging from allusions to later people and concepts in his writings. Be that as it may, this Pseudo-Dionysius, as he is called, described what we might call the "Big Bang of Divine Life" this way:

> God was so touched by the sweet spell of Goodness, Love, and Yearning, that he was drawn from his transcendent throne above all things to dwell within the hearts of all things.... Therefore, on the one hand, they call him the object of Love and Yearning because he is beautiful and good, and, on the other, they call him Yearning and Love because he is the power that leads all things to himself.... He is his own self-revelation ... a reason for yearning.... He is the Good that overflows into creation and that once again returns to himself.[22]

Here is a divine trinity that makes sense — Goodness, Love, and Yearning — for you cannot separate any one of these three from the other two. We yearn for what we perceive as good; we perceive as good what we yearn for; we cannot help loving, in some way, what we yearn for; and we cannot yearn for something we don't love. It is a primordial chicken-and-egg dilemma. But a nice one. We cannot even really affirm which comes first: Goodness, Love, or Yearning. Is something good because we yearn for it; or do we yearn for it because it is good? The same questions can be asked about what we love.

Recalling the Irish words Dúileamh, *dúile,* and *dúlra* (Creator, elements, and nature), we find ourselves in a web of relationships that can only be understood, or understood most sensibly, by accepting the interconnectedness of all created things, including the One Who Made All Things. This recognition does not come easily. That is why mystery schools and sacred initiations have been needed throughout history to prepare and train individuals for this kind of understanding.

Try this. Sit beneath a tree and close your eyes. Think about the trunk against your back. Then begin to say lines like the following, slowly, purposely, intimately, pausing on each line to really experience it.

*I am the tree growing from the soil.*
*I am the soil gathered around the roots.*
*I am the roots searching for water.*
*I am the water flowing through the soil.*
*I am the soil soaking up the water.*
*I am the water seeping into roots.*
*I am the roots sucking up the water.*

Continue going back and forth between root, soil, and water, trying to experience what each yearns for. Then move your awareness up the trunk, the bark, the branches, the leaves, all the way to the wind that blows through them. Try to experience how each element yearns to do what it was created to do, and that in each element's own way, it loves doing what it was created to do, and loves being in contact with the other elements that help it fulfill its own yearning and goodness. Even when that fulfillment is its own destruction and transformation into something else. Do this for as long as you can.

When you have finished, make a leap of faith and say to yourself that what you have just experienced is what the Dúileamh experiences everywhere every day.

# CHAPTER 22

# The Shifting Shapes of God

There is a genre of Celtic poetry called the "boast." A boast usually consists of a litany of statements in which the poet claims to be, or to have been, many things in creation.

The boast of Amergin, an ancient Irish poet, goes like this:

*I am the wind that blows across the sea,*
*I am a wave of the deep,*
*I am the roar of the ocean,*
*I am a hawk on a cliff,*
*I am a stag of seven battles,*
*I am a ray of the sun,*

*I am the greenest of plants,*
*I am a lake on the plain,*
*I am the wildest of boars,*
*I am a salmon in the river,*
*I am a hill of poetry,*
*I am a sword in battle —*
*I can shift my shape like a god.*[23]

The Welsh bard Taliesin boasts of all that he has been with these words:

*I have been in many shapes before I assumed*
  *this present form:*
*I have been the edge of a sword,*
*I have been a drop of rain in the air,*
*I have been a shining star,*
*I have been a letter in a word on a page in a*
  *book,*
*I have been a bridge over threescore rivers,*
*I have been lantern-light for a year and a day,*
*I have been a boat on the sea,*
*I have been a string on a harp,*
*I have been a shout in battle,*
*I have been enchanted in the foam of water —*
*There is nothing in which I have not been.*[24]

These and similar statements of the mystical one-ness between the speaker and creation are not just fanciful lines of poetry. They are expressions of the soul's deepest knowledge; namely, the soul knows the Goodness, Love, and Yearning of all things. Put another way, all things are already, at this very moment, in the soul, yearning for and loving the good for which they were created. As we grow to appreciate how the soul is co-expansive with the length, breadth, and height of the created universe, we discover that the mysteries of creation are already sleeping inside us, waiting to be awakened. In those moments of awakening or enlightenment, we know the yearning of the wind that blows across the sea, the longing of the sea beneath that wind, we know the roaring of the ocean, and the yearning of the hawk for the cliff, and we know how the cliff itself yearns to feel the sharp claws of the hawk.

In such moments, something in us wakes up and we discover that our souls are not tucked away neatly inside our bodies or our minds. It is precisely the other way around. My body and mind are folded into my soul, which brings to me, through my senses, knowledge of the oneness of all created things.

The soul is a shape-shifter simply because the soul is the same "stuff" as the Creator, whose own power and energy well up in all that has been created and continues to be created. God is a shape-shifter. Shape shifting might just be the essential, and only, activity of the universe.

When you sit back against a tree and allow your awareness to drift through the bark, the trunk, roots, soil, rainwater, and so forth . . . when your consciousness drifts into *anything* in nature and experiences it from inside its own Goodness, Love, and Yearning, then you too can boast. But whatever may be the specific words you put into your boast, there is really only one boast, and that is "I am the shifting and shaping of God."

CHAPTER 23

# ΠigΗτ WατcΗiΠG

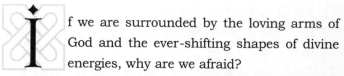f we are surrounded by the loving arms of
God and the ever-shifting shapes of divine
energies, why are we afraid?

I spent a night on the wind-beaten Braunsberg, a
mountain in Hainburg, Austria, the site of an old Celtic
hill settlement. Celtic people had lived there for eight hundred years until Roman armies slaughtered the entire
population in 6 A.D. Nothing has occupied the mountain
since. It is a relatively flat, lonely hilltop, high above the
Danube River, looking eastward to Bratislava, the capital
of Slovakia. A simple plaque commemorates the Celtic
people who lived and died there.

I felt drawn to this mountain on a previous trip to

Austria, and so, on my return, I arranged to spend the night up there, alone with the wind and rain, a small flock of sheep, a modest archaeological dig shut down for the night. And the ghosts. As darkness deepened around me, the wind picked up, blowing the sharp darts of rain fiercely against my skin. I found a declivity among the stones and blasted trees that offered some shelter, but not much, and I hunkered down beneath my rain parka for the night.

At some point, I heard horses' hooves galloping across the hilltop, accompanied by shrilly shouting voices, which I could not understand. I recalled tales of the Wild Hunt, that fierce trooping of spirits that hound the souls of the dead across the sky. The darkness of the night, hostility of the elements, and unfamiliar sounds overcame me, and I panicked. I was tempted to leave, but there was no way to descend in the dark, so I knew I had to survive on my own until dawn, when my friend Erna would return to fetch me in her car.

Before she left me alone for the night, Erna had given me two lemon-sized stones from the Danube as a river gift for protection. So I began grinding them together next to my ear as I lay curled in a fetal position beneath my parka. The raw, gritty drone eventually filled my consciousness, and evolved into what sounded like a comforting song, possibly from Danu herself, the ancient Celtic goddess for whom the river is named. The stone song was soothing. In time, the horses quieted, and the voices that sounded like the screams of lost wanderers subsided. Then one gentler horse appeared and clomped the rocky ground with a hoof as if to bid me follow him. I did, and he led me back in time to a peaceful settlement of men, women, children, animals, huts, and what I assumed were the typical activities and sounds of village life. I fell asleep dreaming deeply into this ancestral past.

My friend Karl spent a night on Knocknarea at the hilltop cairn of Queen Maeve in western Ireland. It was the time of the summer solstice, when the sun barely sets in that northern latitude. As the sun hung over the ocean rim, Karl watched it shoot rainbows into the sky over Sligo before disappearing beneath the sea. Then faces appeared in the twilit darkness, and it began to rain. He wondered why he was there, recalling the advice of a Native American friend back home that if he just showed up, the spirits would tell him what it was all about.

Then a white stone on top of the mound began to glow and beckon. Karl followed it into the mysteries of that ancient tumulus where he had a Druidic vision of "a new fire" and "a new center" for people "who had no fire of their own." In this realm of uncertainty and rain, Karl wondered, "What am I here for?" Around midnight he prayed and the rain stopped. Later he stood up into the dawn, raised a ceremonial sword into the returning sun's rays, and realized, as he put it later, "A Queen was there, the Queen of the Land." And in the brightening daylight, he prayed for his family, friends, and people back home. And he knew why he had come.

Frank, another friend, spent a night in a Pictish grave in Scotland to commune with his Scottish ancestors, a time-honored rite among Gaelic people seeking ancestral wisdom. After sliding down into the grave, he began to hear strange voices, many footsteps, a cough, and a weird clanking sound. He looked deeply with his "visioning eye" and saw what he described as a procession of humanlike beings passing through the mists. He concluded that they might be people of Faery or the ancient Shining Ones who now live in the hollow hills.

After a while, Frank began to hear a music so beautiful that he knew it was the song of the universe, sung by trees, stones, wind, and water. The great song, which he calls the Oran Mór, surrounded him, and he felt a warm feminine spirit presence that he took to be the goddess Brigid encompassing and comforting him. She allayed whatever lingering fear he had.

We get scared. In spite of the encompassing of the Divine Presence and the horizon of the sacred elements that always encircle us and are, in fact, part of our souls, we get scared. We fall into ego fright, that protective warning system of the ego announcing physical threats to the body and psychic attacks against our sense of self.

It is human to be frightened. Or depressed or lonely or angry. As Frank recalls the early hours in the Pictish grave, he was "nervous, cold, and shivering." And yet he was thrilled to be there. This dance of exuberance and terror, of wholeness and separation, of comfort and abandonment — the dance of the dualities — this too is the stuff of soul making.

In some sense we are still children, fumbling through life, frightened by the night, fearful of strange noises, and anxious about new experiences. Even if we are "old" souls, we are still engaged in soul making, for our souls have never lived these unique lives before. What our souls become in this life is open-ended. Standing on the edge of the ancient past and the dawning of a bright or dark or twilit future, these child souls of ours are yearning to grow up.

Curiously, all three of us night watchers felt the need to return to those ancient Gaelic rites of our ancestors. And there in places betwixt and between what we know as time and space, we found the encompassing of Brigid, Danu, Maeve. Perhaps those Mothers of eternal comfort came to us because they knew we were little children, dreaming and delving for visions at ancient burial sites, hoping to recover lost pieces of our terribly young and frightened souls.

# CHAPTER 24

# FAERIES OHIO STYLE

ature is not always safe. Sometimes the elements that comprise nature and are the stuff of our souls can do us great harm. There are stories everywhere about people spending a night on a sacred mountain who do not come down at dawn. Later their bodies are discovered. Or never discovered.

An old Celtic saying warns that a person who spends a night on a holy mountain will become a poet, go crazy, or die. To this day I wonder how Karl survived Knocknarea and I the Braunsberg. Perhaps neither of us has reached his capacity for madness and poetry. So if we plan to do this again, we take our chances. Frank, a wiser man, crawled into the earth, pulled the ghostly shrouds of his ancestors up to his chin, and hoped for the best. If he never woke up in the morning, well at least he was already in a grave.

Nature takes us. When I was a child, I heard tales every springtime about how someone (usually a kid like me) always drowned each summer in the Meramec River, a brown, sluggish stream that meanders around the outskirts of St. Louis and empties into the even browner Mississippi, south of the city. I don't know if the tales were true, or whether they were just scare stories that adults tell to make kids cautious about the old swimming holes each year. Still, I do remember photographs in newspapers of kids who had drowned. Where I now live in New York State, there is an old Lenape story about the Wif-toona-wis, a hateful monster in the Hudson River that eats little children. I've never seen it. We didn't have a monster in St. Louis that I know of, but to this day I think of the Meramec as a dangerous river.

In some parts of the world such tales are told about the spirit of a river or lake who demands a human sacrifice each year. Someone must die. Then the spirit is satisfied. After the dreaded event, no one drowns. Everyone is safe.

One year in early spring I was camping alone in southern Ohio and decided to drive the twenty miles from my campsite to a trailhead that looked promising. The final four or five miles were off the state highway through the wild wooded hollows typical of Appalachia, but the map put out by the Forest Service was excellent.

I followed the lefts and rights, the hills and dips, the paved and unpaved roads, the T-junctions and hidden drives very easily. It was a good map right down to the last eight-tenths of a mile between the last turn and the trailhead's parking area.

I pulled into the empty parking area, locked the car, and headed up the trail. I spent the day wandering through the hills and hollows, and returned to my car just before sunset. It had been a pleasant day. Mine was still the only car in the area.

As I pulled out onto the gravel road, I recalled that the first turn would be in eight-tenths of a mile. It would be a left. Then something weird happened. My mind may have gotten distracted or fallen into a reverie, but after awhile I realized that I had gone quite a ways without seeing the left turn. I turned around, headed back, watching for the road that would now be on the right. Soon I was back at the trailhead. No road. I pulled into the parking area.

I drove back out and tried it again. This time I watched the odometer, and in two miles I had not found a left turn. I saw some roads off to the right, but they were not the one I was looking for. I headed back to the parking area. Then I figured that perhaps I turned the wrong way pulling out of the parking area, so I tried again, this time going in the opposite direction. I came to a crossroads after about a mile, but I knew this was not my turn. I was looking for a T-intersection. I went a little farther, then back to the trailhead. I was quite upset. Virgos don't handle situations like this very well.

At this point, according to my women friends, I suffered the "male curse." I refused to ask directions or look at the map. I had seen a couple homes along the road, even a woman cutting her grass, but the male curse is a dreadful curse. I knew I was right. I did not need to consult the map (in the trunk of the car) because I remembered exactly this eight-tenths of a mile. So I tried again. After about five miles, having not seen a left turn that looked like the one I remembered, I got a chill.

Something creepy dawned on me. Although the day was hot, I began to shiver. Why had I not thought of this before? I headed back to the parking area, both shivering and sweating at the same time. I was never going to get out!

In Ireland they would have said that I stepped on a "stray sod." But in Ohio I had been *driving* on "stray sods" for miles. This was serious. This was classic stuff.

It was Them. They had turned things around.

I remembered an old folk custom to save yourself when this kind of thing happens, but I had never tried it. I had never needed to. You turn your coat or jacket inside out, and somehow that fools Them.

I leaped out of my car, ripped off my T-shirt, turned it inside out, pulled it on, and hopped back into the car. I was both scared and furious. I gripped the steering wheel tightly. I gritted my teeth. I snarled, "Out of my way!" Then I floored it.

I peeled out of the parking area, my eye on the odometer as I raced down the gravel road, dust and stones flying up behind me like a whirlwind. I refused to look at the road. I was going to win this. When the odometer read exactly eight-tenths of a mile, I started to turn left. Then I looked up. It was there! The dirt road!

When I got back out to the state highway, I noticed that I had spent almost an hour trying to get out of that hollow, something that should have taken only fifteen minutes or so. To this day I don't know why They did it. I have several theories, but the one I think is probably the correct one is also the strangest.

Every now and then someone becomes a game, a challenge, a sacrifice.

For a few minutes back there in the dust, I had panicked. I was sure my life was over. This was it. The spirits wanted *me*.

I drove back to my campsite thinking about Einstein and Sila, the famous physicist and Eskimo god, respectively. What can we say to them? Is the universe a friendly place? Should we not be afraid of the universe?

Maybe we can have it both ways. Maybe it is possible to be afraid . . . without being afraid of the universe. I hope so.

# CHAPTER 25

# Where Have All the
# Strawberries Gone?

"Fear is a shape shifter." That's what a woman I will call "Sally" reported after her vision quest in the Catskill Mountains of New York a few summers ago. I had left her at a pleasant spot that she had chosen by a mountain stream where she would pray and fast alone for three days and nights. A pleasant spot, yes, but oh how it was haunted!

When Sally returned to our base camp at the end of her quest, she announced her terrifying discovery. "Every time I overcame my fear, it came back in a different form."

We asked her to explain.

"The first day I was scared that some guy would

stumble upon me and attack me. I worried about that all day until nightfall. Then I was scared that a bear or a wild animal would get me. At dawn I grew anxious again about the male hiker. But then it started to rain. At last, I thought no one will be hiking in the rain. I was safe. But then as the rain continued, I started thinking that maybe the water in the stream would rise and flood my site, or I'd get washed away. So to put my mind at rest, I moved my gear farther up the mountain, away from the stream. Then I worried that if something did happen to me, you wouldn't know where I was because I had moved."

Breaking her fast on a muffin, Sally saw the humor in this. She began to laugh. "I couldn't win! I had to worry about something!"

Fear is indeed a shape-shifter.

Perhaps it is the ogre who haunts the Great Split between the Me and the Not-Me, the demon born in our rupture with the universe. Maybe fear is the result of forgetting that our souls reach to the ends of the earth, that everything that exists is part of us already and somehow familiar.

Perhaps fear arises when we are not in the present moment. When we imagine that a wild animal will eat us later in the night. Or when we notice we are not as comfortable as we were last night at home in our dry, cozy beds.

Perhaps fear is the flip side of excitement. It is excitement without courage. When we are totally engaged, enthused, committed to the thrill of the present moment — and its dangers — we are not afraid of being afraid. Carnival rides play on this excitement, as do horror movies. Some people love them. Yes, we might still be terrified, but it is a terror that excites us and makes us come alive.

Ironically, most of the things I've been afraid of in my life never happened. The same is true of Sally's experience on the vision quest. No dangerous hiker appeared, no bear ate her, the stream did not wash her away, no emergency required me to go find her. The only thing that "got" her was fear itself.

There is a Zen story about a man who was chased by a wild tiger to the edge of a cliff. Standing on the precipice, the man lost his footing and slid down the embankment until he caught himself on an exposed root. He looked down to the raging river hundreds of feet below him. If he climbed back up, the tiger would eat him; if he dropped to the river, he would drown. In fact, the tiger might come down the embankment and get him anyway, or his strength would give out and he would no longer be able to hang from the root. He was terrified.

Then he noticed a wild strawberry growing just inches from his face. He looked up at the tiger; he stared down at the raging river.

Then calmly, he ate the wild strawberry.

# CHAPTER 26

# FEAR AND LOVE

The snarling tiger on the cliff and the raging rapids below make it difficult to conceive of nature as loving and affectionate toward us, as Scottish blessings from the nineteenth century would have us assert. "The love and the affection of the sun be yours, the love and affection of each living creature be yours. You are the pure love of each living creature. You are the pure love of the God of Life."

But the love and affection of the raging river be yours?! You are the pure love of the ravenous tiger?!

We have considered fear to be something that arises when we are not in the present moment, or when the excitement of the moment is not charged with courage, enjoyment, or love. But real danger can lurk in any moment, whether it is accompanied by fear or not, whether we are enjoying that moment or not.

The tiger and the river threaten real physical harm, even death itself, but are they not also the stuff of soul making? Are they not part of my soul seeking acknowledgment, or perhaps parts of my soul seeking fulfillment? And is not my soul, along with the tiger and the river, simply the overflowing of God's Goodness, Love, and Yearning? In other words, the tiger is simply God yearning for what a tiger sees as Good, even if, at this moment, the "good" is to eat me. The river is simply God loving and enjoying the Goodness of swiftly flowing waters, regardless of whether I fall into them or not. Is not my physical body just, unfortunately, in the way of God loving the Goodness for which he yearns?

Well, yes. But that doesn't help me feel any better about dying in the jaws of a tiger or at the bottom of a river, even if the tiger and the river are both God and already part of my soul.

How can we make sense of this? Or if we can't make sense of it, how can we at least learn to live with these sentiments so it *feels* like they make sense?

It is easy for people who do not live *with* nature (possibly you and I) to either romanticize it or demonize it. Since we do not *live with* nature, we *think about* nature. We are concerned about its well-being and the human recklessness that upsets the natural patterns in the world; we find in nature allegories and signs of spiritual truths; or we see in nature a ruthless, amoral engine of destruction that appears to operate without compassion, having little or no compunction about our human welfare.

Spells, charms, prayers, rituals, and offerings to the spirits are the time-honored expressions of people who live *with* nature. They have learned from their intimate daily experience with nature that human beings are not separate from nature, that we must participate in spiritual ways even as we cooperate with nature in physical ways to provide food, shelter, and other necessities. We are obliged to live with nature in a spiritual way, for the obvious reason that we are spiritual beings. To do otherwise is to deny who we are, to deny our own true nature. Earlier people living in closer rhythms with the seasonal changes of nature seemed to have known this. They neither romanticized nor demonized nature but found in nature the same kinds of spiritual forces and energies they found in themselves.

The shaman also knows this. The shaman walks between the worlds, lives in the betwixt and between of various realities. One reality is the tiger and river waiting to destroy us. Another reality is the flow of divine power that animates and permeates all created things, including the tiger, the river, my soul, and everything to the far reaches of the earth. The shaman's role is to keep the threads of these two realities woven together. The thread of appropriate measures and safeguards to avoid physical danger, maintain health, and assure a long life. And the thread that maintains a loving and affectionate relationship with Life Itself. With both threads woven around each other, we may come to understand the mysterious wholeness of a world in which both destructive and loving forces play vital roles.

The way of the shaman is to honor the intimacy among all created things. Sometimes that intimacy is expressed as love and affection, sometimes as death and destruction. Both acts are intimate. Both acts call forth from us, maybe even demand of us, an intimate response.

We contain this paradoxical world within ourselves. We can love and enjoy other beings, and support and enhance their lives, or destroy them. Similarly, other beings can love and enjoy us, and enhance our lives, or destroy us.

Our challenge in life is the shaman's challenge: to balance these two realities, these two truths. How to know in moments of decision which one to choose? To fight or elude the forces that can destroy us? To reach for the forces that offer us health, gladness, and enjoyment?

The man hanging from the root made his choice. He decided he had no time to worry about the reality of death and destruction that awaited him. He simply grabbed the last moment of love and enjoyed it.

# CHAPTER 27

# Nothing So Good
# Has Taken Their Place

In the late nineteenth century men and women in the rural Highlands and islands of western Scotland lived with an intense intimacy with the natural world. Their close physical and spiritual relationship with nature arose from a worldview of such complexity and simplicity that were we to be transported back there, our modern sensibilities would be at a loss to understand the paradoxes of that world. The threads of consciousness that simple men and women found woven through the natural world would seem too complex for our cynical disbeliefs. The daily practice of expressing their love to (and not just *for*) the elements of nature, and receiving love in return, may appear too simpleminded for our overly analyzed theories of human love and affection.

These rural Highlanders structured their days, nights, and seasons by the rhythms of nature, much as their ancestors had. They knew the storm and the wind, the full and dark moons, the freezing ice of winter, the flowering of the glens in summer, and the unpredictable behavior of animals. They neither romanticized nor demonized the forces of nature. They lived with them physically and spiritually.

An old Highland woman reported to an inquiring visitor in the late nineteenth century that the people "had runes which they sang to the spirits dwelling in the sea and in the mountain, in the wind and in the whirlwind, in the lightning, and in the thunder, in the sun and in the moon and in the stars of heaven."[25] These runes — songs, prayers, and blessings — were constantly on their lips as people went about their daily business. "You are the cow of my love," they would say while milking. "You are the heifer of my joy."[26]

Another Highland woman prayed while setting her eggs for hatching: "I will sing my rune and rhyme and go sunwise to the nest of my hen. I will ask for the loving wisdom of God overflowing in offspring, broods, and beasts."[27]

The following blessing for cows as they are taken out to pasture is a remarkable prayer that calls on traditional Christian figures, such as Mary and the archangel Michael, as well as Cormac, who was a semi-historical chieftain, and the ever-mysterious Brigid, who might be goddess or saint or both.

> *The sanctuary of Mary Mother be yours . . .*
> *The protection of shapely Cormac be yours . . .*
> *The fellowship of Brigid of the herds be yours . . .*
> *The fellowship of Michael victorious be yours*
> *In nibbling, in chewing, in munching.*[28]

The Highlander never allowed this kind of roll call of supernatural beings to become too remote from the practicalities of daily life, for the blessing concludes with the same slobbering activities of cows known the world over.

Blessing seed, a man would say, "I will sow the seed, and I will come round with my step, going to the right, the way of the sun. . . . Later I will lift the first cut (of corn) and put it three turns around my head, saying my rune all the while, my back to the airt of the north, my face to the fair sun of power."[29]

Their faith assured them that if they performed their rituals, then when "rough storms come with frowns no suffering nor hardship shall be on us."

Some of these country folk went into a dark closet or shed, some hiked out alone to the leeward side of a hill or into a hidden glen to say their prayers to the spirits: "You are the moon of the seasons, my good friend. I am turning my eyes to you, bending my knee to you, lifting up my hands to you, raising my voice to you."[30]

A few folks, even some quite elderly, walked a mile or more to the seashore so that their voices would be in rhythm with the crashing waves or the lapping water. They wanted their words to be intimately woven into the sounds of nature herself: "You are the moon of the seasons, you are the moon of moons and of blessings."

One crofter explained her practice with these words: "Every creature on the Earth here below and in the ocean beneath and in the air above is giving glory to the great God of the creatures and the worlds . . . and would we be silent?"[31]

We do not live as intimately with nature as did the remote nineteenth-century Scottish Highlanders. Our own lives are embedded in the modern conveniences and technologies that separate so much human activity, thinking, and feeling from the natural world. So in small ways we would do well to find, observe, and celebrate that natural world as it continues to peek into our lives. The sky brightening at dawn through the bedroom window. A birdcall in the middle of the morning. The lengthening afternoon shadows that remind us the sun moves westward. The raindrops rolling down a windowpane. Even the passing landscape as we drive to our demanding destinations.

In small ways try to find the love and affection in each living thing; try to notice the elements of nature looking upon us with their own pure love. Even though it jangles every scientific, rational nerve in your body, try to think of the storm and the whirlwind as somehow deserving your blessing. If we don't do these things, who will? If no one preserves these ancient customs, the Earth will have lost yet another spiritual practice that maintains the loving intimacy between people and the natural world.

Even in the nineteenth century the older Scottish generation saw that the younger people disregarded these customs, thought them foolish, and often made fun of their elders for removing their hats to the moon, or bowing to the sun at sunset, or going down on their knees before the night sky. One elderly person regretted that she didn't see people doing these ancient rites anymore. "The old ways disappeared. Oh, they disappeared indeed," she lamented, "and nothing so good has come to take their place, no, nothing so good has taken their place. Nor ever will."[32]

# CHAPTER 28

# The Strength
# of Heaven

Our estrangement from the natural world may not offer us opportunity to bless cows, eggs, a hearth fire in the morning before work, or the rising of the moon over water. But we could make a traditional prayer for strength and protection attributed to St. Patrick part of our daily spiritual practice or as a reminder of the divine presence that accompanies us in times of fear or danger.

Patrick represented the Roman brand of Christianity that had become the official religion of the Roman Empire. Church leaders, the bishops, modeled their authority on that of the Roman governors who ruled a Europe carved into administrative territories, or provinces.

When the empire fell, the bishops remained, using the towns and cities that had formerly been the administrative seats of the empire as their own seats of power. Roman-style Christianity thus took on an episcopal structure dependent on the towns and surrounding farmlands for financial, political, and social support.

This was the church Patrick hoped to establish in Ireland. As fate would have it, Ireland had never been part of the Roman Empire. Roman armies never invaded. Consequently it lacked the one crucial element for the episcopal system to really work: towns as seats of authority. The Irish still lived in small tribal communities composed of extended families and run by chieftains. The small villages and scattered settlements were more conducive to the loosely knit monastic system of Christianity that had arrived in Ireland a couple centuries before Patrick. These earliest Celtic Christians were the ancestors of the Irish who would settle the Scottish Highlands and islands, who in turn were the ancestors of the people I described in the previous chapter with their charms and blessings for the elements.

Irish chieftains who mistrusted Patrick's church, and the centralized bureaucracy he hoped to establish, opposed him. On one occasion, to avoid hostile warriors, Patrick composed a rune for help and strength, a rune intended to make his men appear as deer so that they could pass undetected (it worked), a rune that has survived into our own era as a remarkable expression of the divine power in the natural elements of the universe. It goes in part like this:

*I arise today with the strength of heaven —*
*Light of sun,*
*Radiance of moon,*
*Splendour of fire,*
*Speed of lightning,*
*Swiftness of wind,*
*Depth of sea,*
*Stability of earth,*
*Firmness of rock.*[33]

These lines are just a fragment of the much longer and more traditional Christian prayer that begins:

*I arise today with a mighty strength,*
*Calling on the Trinity,*
*Believing in the Threeness*
*And witnessing to the Oneness*
*Of the Creator of Creation.*

These lines and the list of elements above are expressions of a Celtic Christianity that never lost that older understanding that spiritual power was one with the elements themselves. Such sentiments should have been jarring to Patrick's Romanized theology, which, over the years, would come to mistrust nature and the spirits of nature. But perhaps he was simply allowing the Celticness he had inherited from his parents to utter forth. Like his Celtic forebears, he knew that divine power is a trinity, a sacred threeness, and yet also a closely and intimately woven unity or oneness of the Creator and Creation.

Patrick called upon the "strength of heaven" and found it, not in some remote celestial paradise far removed from daily life. No, he found it in sun, moon, wind, lightning, sea, fire, soil, and the rock scattered across the countryside like crops, animals, people.

CHAPTER 29

# A Haunting

I am haunted by threeness. Possibly because three, I am told, is a sacred number. But so is five, and seven, and one, and four. By some accounts all numbers are sacred, but I have never been much of a Pythagorean, nor am I quite sure what being a Pythagorean entails. I hated math in school, even before I discovered negative numbers. My natural inclination is not to see the essence of reality as composed of numbers, even though I marvel at musical chords and progressions, nautilus shells, and certain repeatable patterns in flower petals. But numbers as such do not haunt me. *Three* haunts me.

As a young boy trying to understand my Roman

Catholic heritage, I fretted over the Blessed Trinity more than most kids I knew. In those days we called the three persons of this trinity the Father, Son, and Holy Ghost. We were to understand that they were One and Indivisible. And yet Catholic theology had separated them out rather distinctly.

The Father created the universe and was either pleased or displeased by how I treated my younger sisters. The Son became Jesus of Nazareth who saved me from my sins (which might or might not include the way I treated my younger sisters). The Holy Ghost was always a bit weird to wrap your mind around. Most ghosts are. There were pictures of the Holy Ghost as a dove hanging over Jesus' head when he was baptized in the River Jordan or as flaming tongues hanging over the apostles' heads on Pentecost. The Holy Ghost seemed to be always hovering a little bit above your head. But we were to understand that this third person was not a dove really, nor were we to believe that every dove we saw was the Holy Ghost. As it turned out, I never saw a flaming tongue, so I didn't worry much about that. The Holy Ghost didn't seem to have any connection to how I treated my sisters, and for that reason I sort of cottoned to him. But he didn't seem to have much connection to *anything* in my life.

I was also obsessed in my youth with fairness (although my sisters tell a different story). I believed that if I were really going to be spiritual, I should give each of these three persons equal time in my prayers and devotions. I didn't. There were more stories about Jesus of Nazareth than the others, and since he was an actual historical man, you could glide over the "Second Person of the Blessed Trinity" aspect of his existence. I liked him. He was a great teacher, storyteller, and healer. He said some cool things. I didn't pay too much attention to his mysterious role as the "Word of God" existing before all time. But I did occasionally wonder if I was hurting my case, spiritually speaking, by not praying equally to the Father and Holy Ghost.

In college I discovered Plato, and quickly lost him. He too had a nifty idea about the threeness of the Godhead, but it didn't stick in my head for very long. Possibly because it was the '60s, and sex, drugs, and rock 'n' roll had more kick to them. Plato's trinity — the One, the Divine Mind, and the All-Soul — was mind-numbingly logical and abstract, and I was into the Romantic poets, beer busts, and street protests, all of which were more fun than hanging out with Platonic ideal forms.

Then as the neo-pagan movement got off and running, I discovered the Triple Goddess: the maiden, mother, and crone. This made a lot of sense, and still does, as I see the Mothers of Life almost everywhere. And it stands to reason that at times this Great Goddess is young and full of potential, free and wild, and untamable. At other times she is truly a mother with responsibilities and children to care for. And there is no avoiding encounters with her as the tough, no-nonsense, wise old woman, ever ready to remind us that we are going to die and we'd better get used to the idea.

In Celtic lore the goddess Brigid is a triple goddess also, but her tripleness is a little more specialized. She is the patron of poetry, healing, and metalwork. It takes a little reflection to see how these three seemingly disconnected activities fall into the bailiwick of one female spirit, but Brigid is also the power of eternal fire and the returning life warmth of spring. She is the burning energy at the heart of poetry, healing, and metalwork. She is the fire of inspiration that sets the poet's head aflame with a yearning to describe new visions. She is the proper balance of warmth and cold, both within the body and without, that maintains health. And her fire creates and shapes metal; her energy is at the heart of all technology. Clearly Brigid is a trinity of important and specific human experiences.

But none of these trinities explains the haunting. Only the Irish word *cruthaitheoir* explains it.

# CHAPTER 30

# Iɴ ᴛʜᴇ ɴᴏ-Bᴇɢɪɴɴɪɴɢ

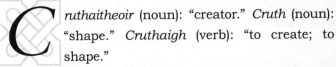

*ruthaitheoir* (noun): "creator." *Cruth* (noun): "shape." *Cruthaigh* (verb): "to create; to shape."

Not being a speaker of Irish, I never get to say these words. I never use them in conversation. In fact, I'm somewhat relieved that I don't have to, since I find them a bit intimidating. I am not absolutely sure I can pronounce them correctly. I know them only as facts, similar to the dates of Leonardo da Vinci's life (1452–1519) or the symbol for water ($H_2O$), two facts that, like the Irish words, I seldom drop into my conversation.

But these three words haunt my thoughts, and

they lift my "trinitarian haunting" to new levels of excitement, mystery, and, paradoxically, comfort.

The Irish word for "create" comes from the root-word for "shape." In English *create* implies making something out of nothing. In fact, the very first definition in *Webster's Dictionary* is "to bring into existence." Only in the second definition do we get the idea of shaping: "to invest with a new form." The Irish definition emphasizes the idea that creation is about shaping. Now you can't shape something that doesn't already exist. That's what shaping means: you take something like clay, wood, or mud, and give it a new form.

One of the mysteries of Celtic history is the absence of creation myths. Most cultures have them — wonderful, bizarre, mind-bending, soul-stretching accounts of how this marvelous and mysterious universe came to be. A sampling: The cosmos was created from the body of a Giant, or the blood of a God, or the flesh of a Goddess; or it was hatched from a cosmic Egg, or thought into existence by an original Mind, or uttered forth as the primordial word from a divine Voice. The world's creation myths do not agree with each other, and for that reason they challenge our sense of mystery. They inspire us to dream deep dreams and imagine far out and far back to ancient beginnings.

Did none of this interest the Celtic peoples?

There are two theories about the absence of creation stories among the Celts. One is that they had them but they've been lost. According to this theory, the early Irish scribes who wrote down other Celtic myths and tales did not, for some reason, preserve origin stories. But why not? It's true the early monks and scribes were Christian, but they were obsessively curious about other pagan tales, and they preserved them. Even if they saw Celtic creation myths as competition with the Genesis account, they could have "cleaned" them up, given them a Christian spin, as they did other myths, and we'd have them today. If they had turned them into bad jokes, we'd at least have them.

The other theory is that the Celts never had creation stories. They saw the universe, not as something that came into existence at some point in time, or before time, but as something that just is, has always been, and always will be. The universe is eternal. If there is a Creator, this eternal Being has always been creating the world and everything that exists. There was never a time when All of This Life did not exist. Creation, then, is not a question of making something out of nothing, but shaping and reshaping eternal "stuff."

And what is the nature of this "stuff"?

If I might extrapolate a possible, and very personal, answer from bits and pieces of information from Celtic lore, the nature of this stuff is none other than the Creator's *own* stuff. This eternal, divine, ever-shaping Being's own Essence is the essence of what we call creation. We are shaped from the Creator's own Soul.

So here's the Trinity:

The Shaper of Life. The Shape of Life. The Shaping of Life.

These Three are truly One and Indivisible. No one of

these three can exist without the other two. The entire universe is simply a Divine Shaper shaping shapes. And the shapes, or Shape, is also this Great Divine Life. And the Shaping activity itself is the same Great Creative Being, for that is what this Creator does and therefore is. There is nothing more.

This Sacred Three is always present to us. Indeed, we are part of the Shaper and the Shapes and the Shaping.

The great encompassing or encircling of divine power that we have been considering from different angles throughout this book is none other than the encircling of the Shaper of Life and the Shapes of Life and the ever ongoing, eternal Shaping of Life. There is no end to it.

And here's a prayer to these Three:

*Shaper of Life, above me and below. Shaper of Life, before me as I go. Shaper of Life, at my sides, and I know that You circle me around and around and around.*

*Shape of Life, above me and below. Shape of Life, before me as I go. Shape of Life, at my sides, and I know that You circle me around and around and around.*

*Shaping of Life, above me and below. Shaping of Life, before me as I go. Shaping of Life, at my sides, and I know that you circle me around and around and around.*

*Sacred Three, above me and below. Sacred Three,*
*before me as I go. Sacred Three, at my sides,*
*and I know that you circle me around and*
*round and around.*

# CHAPTER 31

# YEARNING
FOR THE WIND

In the early twentieth century, Ella Young, an Irish writer and mystic, wrote personal versions of the old Celtic myths. In *Celtic Wonder-Tales,* she alludes to the healing power of the wind. In one story the three sons of Tuireann, dispirited in a foreign land, feel a "very soft and gentle wind" that came out of Ireland. "There was so much healing in its touch," wrote Young, "that they rose up and stood on their feet" renewed in spirit.[34] On another occasion, "the Earth sent a little wind" to another character in the story as a messenger about his father's murder. He feels the wind touch his face, eyelids, hair, hand; and he "knew the wind had come for him," so he followed it, and it took him to the place where his father had been slain and buried.[35]

In Celtic folklore there are tales of healing winds coming to cure an illness or revive the dead, or faery winds coming to calm and soothe a person or an animal (even though it may have been a faery wind that caused the problem in the first place!). We find the same idea in an old Chippewa saying: "Sometimes I go around feeling sorry for myself and all the while I am being carried by the wind across the sky."

Irish visionary George Russell, who wrote under the pen name A. E., noted that when we go outside into nature, "the Great Spirit whose home is in the vast becomes for us a moving glamour in the heavens . . . and the air we breathe is like wine poured for us by some heavenly cupbearer."[36] He also suggested that the visible world is like a curtain "blown and stirred by winds behind it."[37]

Russell longed for the Mothers to reveal themselves to him. He asked, "Would the Mother of us all receive me again as one of her children? Would the winds with wandering voices be, as before, the evangelists of her love?" His custom was to go outside "over the dark ridges to the place of rocks . . . and let the coolness of the night chill and still the fiery dust in the brain" while he waited to hear "the shyest breathing of the Everlasting within my soul." There he found healing, restoration, and a renewed spirit to uphold his courage and belief in the invisible realms behind the wind.

Try this yourself. Go outside and sit down quietly

when you feel dispirited or troubled by some problem in life. Even if there doesn't seem to be any air stirring, close your eyes, sit still, and become sensitive to the quality of the atmosphere all around your body. Make prayers to the wind to come and heal you. Make your prayer ardent and heartfelt, fully trusting in the spirit of the wind to respond. Repeat your request until you feel a breeze. It might be very subtle, a simple coolness on one side of your body. But something will shift in the air around you. You will feel it. It might even become a dramatic gust that blows strongly for a lengthy period of time.

As the wind blows, be appreciative, express your gratitude for this healing that comes from the invisible realms of the atmosphere to refresh you. Sit in the wind, enjoy it, listen to what it has to tell you. In the wind you can hear the voice of the Earth breathing, telling you pieces of her ancient story so that you can go back into your life, assured that the Earth has a deep and abiding fondness for you.

When the wind dies down, or you feel you have had enough, go back to your tasks, remembering that part of your soul is still being carried by the wind across the sky. In the words of the Welsh shaman and mystic Taliesin, "The ardent soul shall be voyaging through the clouds with the children of angels."[38]

# CHAPTER 32

# The Coldest Beltane

I arrived in Fairbanks, Alaska, on April 29, two days before Beltane, the traditional start of the Celtic summer. The ice on the Chena and Tanana Rivers had just broken the day before I arrived, and some local citizen had won big money.

In autumn when the rivers freeze, a tripod is placed on the ice. A trip wire is connected from the tripod in the middle of the river to a clock on shore, and when the river thaws, the tripod falls into the water, trips the line, and stops the clock. The exact hour and minute are duly recorded. The lucky person who bet closest to the exact day, hour, and minute wins the pot.

Throughout most of the Lower Forty-eight states,

rivers and lakes have long since thawed by May 1, and spring has been officially around, by our calendar, since the March equinox. So all bets are off. But Alaska warps one's sense of time and season.

I had come to meet with people interested in Celtic practices, and so we could hardly let the traditional Beltane fire go unlit or the stories of Beltane go untold. My visit was one of those occasions I could best describe as "it doesn't get any better than this," for I got to tell an old Irish story about the "Coldest Beltane" on Beltane itself with the cold spring wind howling through the deep leafless woods north of Fairbanks.

The Irish tale is about a time many generations ago when May 1 was frightfully cold in Ireland. Everyone wondered if there had ever been a Beltane colder than that one. I take some liberties with the old myth, and suggest that no one wanted to venture outdoors to light the Beltane fires but preferred to huddle inside by the hearth. The god Aengus thinks this situation entirely unseemly and takes matters into his own hands. He would find out if there had ever been a colder Beltane, and if there had been, it would reassure the shivering Irish people that they could survive the current one. So he goes to ask the Oldest Animals, the ones recognized in this myth and other legends as having the longest memories.

Eagle remembers a colder Beltane when Hawk, hungry because he could not find any food, ate one of her chicks and took its place in the nest to stay warm. But she tells Aengus to check it out with Blackbird, who cannot recall a colder Beltane and sends him to Stag. Stag recommends that the god find Salmon, for Salmon has the oldest memory and is the wisest of all.

Aengus finds the Salmon of Wisdom, swimming furiously in a lake to keep warm. He does indeed recall a colder Beltane, when the river he was swimming in froze, and he was unable to move, with only his head poking above the surface of the iced-over water. Hawk, hungry as usual, pecked out one of Salmon's eyes and ate it. Yes, said Salmon, remembering that tragic day eons and eons ago, there was a colder Beltane than the present one.

So Aengus returned, summoned the frightened people from their cottages, and assured them they would not freeze, for their ancestors had survived the coldest Beltane of them all. They lit the fires and drove the cattle between them to purge the beasts of winter ills. Next, men and women, young and old, leaped the fires to renew the vigor of their loins, the fertility of the earth, and the vitality of the coming summer. Then the earth warmed up, responding to their festive fires. And in the ancient tradition of their ancestors, they spent the night making love deep in the greenwood, and all was as it should be.

After I told the story we went out into the evening to light our Beltane fire. But being so far north, the sky was still light. The evening was bright and chilly. Snow lay on the ground. We huddled in parkas and gloves, scarves wrapped tightly around our necks. We stamped our feet to keep warm. As we lit the fire, it began to snow quite heavily. We sang songs, drummed, and waited for the first brave person to jump through the flames. Needless to say, I was quite disoriented. My Beltane celebrations in New York State are among apple blossoms and beneath dark skies shimmering with a myriad of stars. Peepers chirp, and the evening is warm and pleasant. In Alaska I was cold.

Jumping through fire is always risky and somewhat off-putting. At home we would fear singeing our skin or hair. But around that Alaskan fire people worried, not about their skin, but about their coats, gloves, and stocking caps. In addition, the cold, snowy night created another danger: slipping on ice either when springing forth into the flames or when landing on the far side. For beneath our feet, the snow had melted as we stamped around the edge of the fire, and our shuffling packed the slush down until it refroze on the cold ground. The elements of both winter and summer challenged us: fire, ice, slush.

Eventually a young man, who had "mushed his dogs" only a few days earlier, stepped back, took a running leap, and sailed through the fire unharmed. He landed on the slippery ground, slid a few feet, and swiveled like a top to keep his balance. He survived the jump and did not collapse in the snow. Then we all leaped across the Beltane fire. To paraphrase Shakespeare's Richard III, was ever summer in such humor wooed? Was ever summer in such humor won?

We always live with edges. Our lives are circumscribed in many ways, by place, time, opportunity, landscape, skill, art, health. We have limits and know them. Some people would say it is wisdom to live within your limitations. But hermits and spiritual seekers have thought otherwise. They retreated to deserts, mountaintops, and the trackless wilderness to escape those limits. They have stayed up all night, outdoors, exposed to the fiercest elements to pray and be alone with the Divine. By leaving the known boundaries behind, they hoped to push beyond the very edges of the body itself, ever outward into the soul and perhaps even beyond the soul if that is possible. To know the soul as edgeless, limitless, eternal. To realize that we transcend any physical boundary of time or place.

While most of us cannot build a hermitage on the edge of the earth, we can find it in the smaller regions of our lives. Wherever edges shift, whenever borders are skewed, whenever the unthinkable happens. When it snows on Beltane. When we lose a baby chick or an eye to Hawk. When the Divine Spirit of the universe calls us to sufferings for which we are unprepared, our predictable, comfortable world will seem totally lost. We will be frozen in surprise or sorrow. Then we risk everything venturing into the unknown. At such times, it helps to know that our ancestors have journeyed into these regions before us, that others in times long past have survived.

We discover that we can indeed leap the Beltane fire in winter coats, land on the ice beyond the flames, slide through slush, and welcome summer, not by making love in the greenwood perhaps, but by licking snowflakes from our frozen, shivering lips.

# CHAPTER 33

# The Finest Music in All the World

So what if Beltane is freezing? The unpredictability of nature is part of the so-called laws of nature, and they include exceptions, spontaneity, surprises, and disappointments. We engage in seasonal rituals not to control nature but to celebrate and participate with it. We need to be flexible and find reasons to celebrate and continue participating even when nature, not matching our expectations, seems to let us down.

We are always yearning for something good, something more, something different. Hardly a day goes by that we are not needing something that we don't have. We may be desperately hoping for the wind to blow our souls across the sky, and all we get is a funky little breeze that merely tickles our skin. In such moments we would rather be anywhere than where we are, doing anything other than what we are doing, being anyone other than who we are.

In recent years Ram Dass's expression "Be Here Now" has become popular as a way of being present and focused on the moment and place where you are. It is a wise and important teaching. But what are we supposed to *do* here and now? How do we handle the dilemmas and disappointments of here and now, the pain and sorrow in the present suffering? Assuming our faith does not desert us completely, as during the dark night of the soul, we might try remembering a practice that comes out of Irish folklore.

Once Finn MacCool and his hunters were discussing the "finest music in all the world." The question was posed as a riddle. What is the finest music in the world? One hunter said it was the sound of a stag belling across the lake. Another said it was the sound of rain falling on leaves. The laughter of a young girl, suggested one of them. The sound of dogs yelping during the chase, or water falling over stone, or the wind in the grass. Each hunter had a candidate for the finest music in the world.

Then they asked Finn what he thought it was. He answered, "The finest music in all the world is the music of what is happening."

Is this not a version of Be Here Now? The music of what is happening pulls our attention into the present moment. But then how do we respond? If the present is enjoyable, it is not hard to hear the music as fine and good. But what if the moment is one of suffering, disappointment, loss, boredom, rejection, pain? What Finn is suggesting, I think, is not that the present moment is always pleasurable or enjoyable. He is asking us to look and listen *beyond* the facts of the moment. He calls our attention to another reality that transcends the present but for which the present is the entry. It is a reality of greater significance than what the present moment seems to hold. And it is *that* which produces the finest music in the world.

But what is this other reality, this other music? It is truly otherworldly music — strains of harmony that come from beyond, from eternity. It has been called heavenly music, the choirs of angels, the music of the spheres, and the faery music from the Hollow Hills, the Oran Mór. Hearing it requires an inner ear, a way of listening with the soul. Hearing it is not always easy. Sometimes we feel as if there is nothing but a dry, windless silence — what mystics have called the "silence of God." But they have also taught that God's silence is really an incapacity on our part to hear.

Try this the next time you are discouraged, bored, disappointed, or even in great pain because of your own suffering or the suffering of others. Pause and listen, not with your ears but with your soul. Ask to be pulled even deeper into the moment, but in such a way that the sorrow or pain makes a kind of sense. Listen for a word, a phrase, or a snatch of melody that says your life has greater scope than the present trouble, that the pain of the moment is like an important minor note in a larger symphony of great beauty.

If you hear nothing but a great silence, recall that there is always heavenly and otherworldly music around you whether you hear it or not. Your inability to hear it at the moment does not invalidate it; the silence that surrounds you does not drown out this music, for it is stronger and more eternal than you. You may feel helpless and discouraged, perhaps, but continue doing "what is happening" as you remind yourself over and over, as long as it takes, that there is music in this. It plays, it sings.

Continue to participate in what you are doing, remembering that in some mysterious way — even though you are not able to appreciate it at the moment — this is the finest music in all the world.

# CHAPTER 34

# Face East

Sometimes we just can't hear the music of the present moment no matter how hard we listen. Sometimes we can't see our way out of a present dilemma no matter how hard we look. What can be done?

The wisdom of the Irish airts, or directions, provides an approach for keeping the wheel of our lives turning even when we feel stuck. Recall the qualities of the four directions. In the north is battle; in the east is prosperity; in the south is music; in the west is vision.

The Gaelic languages contain a hidden clue for moving appropriately through these four areas of your life.

The Irish word for east, *oirthear,* contains the root *oir,* which implies "fit, suitable, ready, prepared." It is "fitting" to begin by facing east, which places the north on your left, the south on your right, the west behind you.

The word for south is *deisceart,* which contains the root *deis,* from which comes *deiseal,* meaning "to the right" or "in the right-hand direction." It also means "sunwise." Southward, to your right, is the daily route of the sun as it journeys to its evening setting in the west.

The word for north, *tuaisceart,* contains the root *tua.* The related word *tuathal* means "to go against the sun." It also means "to go in the wrong direction, to blunder, to make a mistake, to go the wrong way."

What this orientation suggests is that the rising sun — bringing light, warmth, growth, nurturance, and prosperity — fits and readies you for the day to come. The Irish word for prosperity, *bláth,* also means blossoming. Face east to blossom and grow strong. Then follow the sun toward the right, toward the south, where there is music. If you turn left, or northward, you expose yourself to battle, struggle, and conflict. The sun never swings through the north on its westward journey each day.

The word for west, *iarthar,* is built from the root *iar,* which means "behind" or "at the back" — the place where the west is when you face east. In the morning as you greet the sunrise, the future lies, not before you, but behind you. You cannot see where you are going. It is invisible. The future requires vision, faith, an ability to see what is not yet apparent.

Our destiny is always, in some sense, invisible. Ultimately, death, our final Earthly destiny, will take us deep into the invisible realms of spirit. But even on a daily basis, we are uncertain where we will be at sunset, how we will feel, what will be happening. And yet, the "music of what is happening" is what will be happening. To commit ourselves to hearing that music means to turn willingly and gladly toward the right, toward the south, and through the place of music. We cannot or should not stand frozen facing east, letting fear or anxiety or the unknown paralyze us.

Only with great reluctance, when it cannot be avoided, do we turn to the north, the place of conflict and struggle. Yet every day contains some element of struggle for most people. To work hard, make a living, build a home, become prosperous, and share the good things of life with those you love is often hard. No flower blossoms easily, each struggles into life, where it immediately begins to die. Such is also our fate. And yet, each day there is a reminder and an orientation that say our lives — including the struggles — have meaning.

Each day we can begin by facing east, making our prayers to the Sun of Suns to lead us away from battle and into the music, laughter, and enjoyment of life, where we may hope to hear the finest music in the world. And as we slowly turn through these melodies of the day, we begin to see our destination. The west takes shape. Evening arrives, and with it perhaps, the vision of a better day to come.

# CHAPTER 35

# SKY TALK

I sat down in the airplane next to a man and woman whom I suspected from their similar clothing style (bright and clean) and similar posture (stiff) to be husband and wife. They were. As I settled down in my aisle seat, I also got the distinct impression that they might be conservative church people. Don't ask how I knew that. Sometimes I'm psychic. I usually don't like to talk to people on airplanes, and on this particular day I was not in the mood to chat up strangers, especially church people who often seem to be trying to convert you, so I retreated into myself. I pulled out a magazine and began to read intensely. I hoped that my own body language clearly indicated Leave Me Alone!

Eventually, though, my curiosity got the better of me. Both of them were reading, and I have a minor addiction to knowing what other people read. So I decided to use what I call my "getting-more-comfortable squirm," during which I can glance furtively into my neighbors' laps and find out what they are reading. I began the squirm. She, sitting by the window, was reading a well-worn Bible. Aha! He, next to me, held a book with a title something like *Thirty Days to Better Sermons*.

I halted in mid-squirm, feeling exposed and naked. I feared that, since I had clearly lowered my magazine, they would take the opportunity to open a conversation. He was probably good at this. I quickly turned a page, rattling the magazine as loudly as I could to announce I had not stopped reading, and withdrew even deeper into my seat; I tried to radiate ever greater intensity and concentration on the article.

The first couple hours went well. Then I went back to the lavatory, leaving the magazine on my seat. It was the current issue of *Shaman's Drum*.

When I returned, the minister politely leaned over and said, "Excuse me, but my wife couldn't help but notice your magazine. Would you mind if she looked at it?"

Over the years *Shaman's Drum* has had many eye-catching covers. Often they depict indigenous shamans in various ritual or healing postures, dances, and trances, as well as shamanic paraphernalia such as drums, rattles, masks, shields, feathers, and bones. Occasionally the artwork on the covers shows ancient deities and spirits, Neolithic rock drawings, skulls, half-human, half-animal beings, and exotic tribal motifs from various cultures. What they all have in common, I suppose, is that to conservative Christians they scream "PAGAN!"

As luck would have it, the cover on the current issue was a real screamer.

"No, not at all," I said, smiling affably, offering the magazine to the minister, who quickly passed it on to his wife. She riffled through it, holding it with her fingertips, as if it had just been lifted, dripping, from a swamp in the Amazon.

"What is shamanism?" she asked with tight lips and a fierce squint, leaning forward and looking around her husband, who had put down his book on goosing up sermons to listen. I suspected he put her up to this.

Over the years I've developed various answers to this question, selecting the one that I think would be appropriate for the questioner and the amount of time available. This was going to be a long flight. But, prudently, I chose my shortest reply, emphasizing spiritual healing. I actually said the phrase "spiritual healing," hoping it would allay their fears.

"What spirits?" she asked. She was not going to be caught off guard.

Again, I have a selection of answers to that one. But some devil got in me, and I chose the one they probably did not want to hear. "Animals, birds, rocks, all the elements — earth, air, fire, water — land spirits and nature spirits, the seasons, the ancestors." I made it sound like there were lots. Well, there are. But I knew it was the

Coyote energy rising in me. I tightened my seat belt. This was going to be a bumpy flight.

"We believe in the one, true God." She said this triumphantly, and pointed upward with her index finger toward the overhead rack. I'm sure she meant Heaven, not the trapdoor through which the oxygen masks fall if cabin pressure fails.

"What god do you believe in?" she asked suspiciously.

"The One who made us," I answered. It wasn't the place to drag out my personal concept of the Trinity as the Shaper of Life, the Shape of Life, and the Shaping of Life, based on a complicated Irish word for Creator, so I didn't. But I pointed downward. She frowned when (as the Irish put it) confusion came upon her. She clearly understood my gesture to complement, or perhaps contradict, her own, but she didn't totally comprehend my meaning.

She pointed upward again, smiling competitively. "Up there," she announced.

"Down there," I countered.

"Heaven," she whispered sweetly and reverently.

"The Earth," I replied with great devotion.

She thanked me and handed *Shaman's Drum* back across her husband.

"The little woman's always curious," he said to me, and went back to his sermons.

I went back to the article about the serpents of healing.

The rest of the flight was uneventful.

## CHAPTER 36

# What's a Heaven For?

My discussion with the church woman on the airplane occurs countless times a day all around the world wherever men and women talk openly about God. Basically we were expressing different views on the whereabouts of God. The two classic positions on this issue are transcendence and immanence. The question might be put this way: Is God a transcendent God in a heaven, far removed from Earth, occasionally manifesting on a remote mountaintop? Or is God immanently present in the daily dripping and oozing of life on Earth wherever that life appears? Reasonable people have held reasonable arguments for both sides and have reasonably disagreed.

A question related to this is: Did creation occur once and for all in some *illo tempore,* dreamtime, Garden of Eden, or time-before-time, or is creation an ongoing process, an evolutionary event that requires the Creator's continual engagement and activity? Put another way, did God create us eons ago and now waits, uninvolved, until some miracle needs to occur? Or is God creatively working in creation minute by minute?

The third-century Celtic warlord Brennus, who invaded the sacred precincts at Delphi in Greece, would probably not appear on any rational Greek's list of top-ten "great theological thinkers." But I would put him rather high up on mine, if not for original thinking then for courage in expressing what he thought about some of these divine matters.

Brennus led an army of Celtic warriors into Greece to plunder and loot. Hearing there was a lot of booty at the Temple of Apollo at Delphi, where the famed oracle dispensed her wisdom to avid seekers, Brennus invaded in 278 B.C. Curiously, there is no archaeological evidence that Delphi was ever looted, yet the story about the Celtic invasion appears in several ancient histories. From these we get Brennus's insightful comebacks to important questions about divinity, questions being asked both then and now, akin to the issue of whether God's in his Heaven and all's right with the world.

When confronted with the possibility that the gods might be offended if Brennus's army sacked the temple for its reputed treasury of gold, the warrior replied, "The gods don't need treasure since they bestow treasures so liberally on us every day." Some might argue that his answer was a bit self-serving, but it accurately reflected a persistent Celtic belief: the gracious generosity of God.

Recall that east is the place of prosperity, the direction rich with the rays from the rising sun that brings warmth and life to all things. The Gaelic word for "prosperity" also means "blossoming." The gifts of God are as bountiful as the lilies of the field, which neither toil nor spin and yet are endowed by the Creator with a radiance unlike any other. I think Brennus would have understood this idea.

Brennus's other reply concerned the magnificent statues of gods and goddesses that lined the precinct of the temple. Like millions of tourists after him, he was awestruck by the grandeur of Greek sculpture. He asked who these strong, beautiful, good-looking men and women might be. "Those are their gods," he was told. Whereupon he laughed and said, "Gods don't look like that!"

His self-assurance sprang from a Celtic tradition of not depicting gods and goddesses in human form. Only after contact with Roman civilization did Celtic artisans begin to copy Roman artists and sculpt images of the gods as human beings. It was inconceivable to Brennus that the idea of Deity could be expressed in human form, or in any man-made sculpture, for that matter. To the Celtic imagination, divine power is wild, unlimited, cosmic, shape shifting, and everywhere, especially in the grand and mysterious forces of nature. The gods are in the trees, springs, rocks, and mountains. This power cannot be contained in a statue! Earlier we saw how the same notion popped up in St. Patrick's prayer for the "strength of heaven" that he found in the sun, moon, fire, wind, lightning, sea, earth, and rock. How can this kind of energy be depicted in a mere human body?

The church woman pointed up to Heaven; I pointed down to Earth. We were both right. The Creator is both transcendent and immanent. I wonder if she went back to her Bible, muttering to herself, Brennus-like, "God's not down there!" As for me, my mind wandered elsewhere.

Perhaps, I thought, in airplanes we really should think of God as being in the overhead rack with the oxygen masks. After all, God can be found in shamans' masks of beaks, antlers, horns, fangs, and feathers. As well as in the birds and animals from which those elements come. Surely, it seems reasonable to also find God in oxygen masks and air filters, reading lights, seat belts, wind currents, wings, and jet fuel. At thirty-five thousand feet, these are treasures enough and a kind of miracle.

I had thought about suggesting this to the couple next to me that day, but I didn't want to start something.

CHAPTER 37

# Soul Stuffing

There are two magnificent descriptions in Gaelic literature of the Creator's work in shaping the universe. The one is St. Patrick's answer to two women, possibly studying Druidism, who were curious about the new missionary's God. They asked him, "Where is this God's dwelling? How can he be seen? How can he be found?"

Patrick answered,

Our God is the God of all people, God of Heaven and Earth, of sea and river, of sun and moon and the stars, of the lofty mountains and the lowly valleys. He is over heaven and in heaven and under heaven, he has his dwelling in heaven and earth and sea and in all the things that are in them.

He inspires all things, he quickens all things, he is over all things, he supports all things. He makes the light of the sun to shine; he furnishes the light of the light; he surrounds the moon and stars; he has put springs in the dry land and placed dry islands in the seas.[39]

Clearly we see here a divine power actively engaged in the present world, dwelling in all things, keeping them alive and vibrant, seeing to it that they do what they were created to do. This is not a remote or transcendent Creator but a Mystery that permeates all creation.

Another early account of the creation of the universe, coming from a ninth-century work, shows the Creator as a divine Shaper, molding, hewing, fashioning the universe out of primordial matter. As in so many of these early works, the author refers to the Creator as "King." This term had different connotations in the centuries before government became centralized and monarchical as we know it. *King* was more akin to *chief,* the admired and respected leader who could claim authority because he or she excelled beyond all others.

The ninth-century poem begins:

*My own King of the pure heavens . . . who*
*created the folded world, my King ever-living,*
*ever victorious.*

*King above the elements, surpassing the sun,*
*above the ocean depths. King in the south*
*and the north, in the west and east . . .*

*King of the Mysteries who was and is, before*
*the elements, before the ages . . . without*
*beginning, without end . . . who created*
*lustrous heaven . . . and the Earth with its*
*multitudinous delights, strong, powerful,*
*stable . . .*

*King who made the noble brightness, and the*
*darkness with its gloom; the one, the*
*perfect day; the other, the perfect night.*

*King who fashioned the vast deeps out of the*
*primary stuff of the elements and the*
*formless mass . . . who formed out of it*
*each element, both tempestuous and*
*serene, both animate and inanimate.*

*King who hewed gloriously, with energy, out*
*of the very shapely primal stuff, the heavy,*
*round Earth . . . who shaped in the circle of*
*the firmament the globe, fashioned like a*
*goodly apple, truly round . . .*

*King who formed the fresh masses about the*
*Earth, the very smooth currents above the*

*world of the chill, watery air... who sifted*
*the cold excellent water on the Earth-mass*
*of the noble cliffs into rills, with deep*
*pools of streams."[40]* .

My favorite line from this passage is "King who hewed gloriously, with energy, out of the very shapely primal stuff." I can see this King, more a carpenter, sculptor, or plain laborer than a monarch, exerting power and skill, art and creativity, "gloriously" enjoying the work of creation, of giving shape to everything that makes up "our lives." In some way that I may never understand completely, I am a descendant of "very shapely primal stuff." This is my ancestral lineage.

And what is this stuff? It is not just the physical elements that make up nature, nor those same elements as they compose my present body, nor those very elements as they dwell in my far-reaching soul.

The stuff itself is soul. It is soul stuff.

And in some way, this divine Shaper is shaping, hewing, making, forming, fashioning, supporting, lightening and darkening, and always quickening and stuffing — with divine energy — my very soul.

In the world. In our souls. This is where the Creator dwells, lives, can be seen, and is found.

# CHAPTER 38

# A Riddle

We sense there are invisible Powers above, below, and around us. At times we sense they are Mothers, birthing into life the world and its many children. Particularly in May, the month that Catholics dedicate to Mary, we see this tremendous resurgence and renewal of life everywhere. Some strong Power of Motherhood stands behind the budding, blossoming, hatching, and emerging of young life as spring bursts upon the land each year.

There is an old Celtic riddle that asks, "Who is the birth that was never born, and never will be?"

I don't know if there is one correct answer to this, or many, or perhaps none. But here is my stab at it.

The answer is the Old Irish word *tuirigin*. A ninth-century glossary defines *tuirigin* as:

> an overtaking birth...a successive birth that passes from every nature into another...a transitory birth that has coursed the expanse of nature from Adam and marvelously goes through all time to the world's end. It brings a nature of one birth to each authentic thing as far as the lone last individual.[41]

*Tuirigin* was an archaic term in the ninth century, and people were not using it very much, and I have not found it in modern Gaelic dictionaries. The long, rambling definition above suggests that it was a mystical term, imbued with great cosmic significance. I wish we still used it. There are, however, two modern Gaelic words that come from the root syllables of *tuirigin*.

*Turas* means "journey or pilgrimage." Today in Ireland a *turas* is the circuit that people make around sacred stations at various times of the year. Often the *turas* is made barefoot and requires walking several miles to cover all the sacred statues, stones, wells, trees, and churches that are the stations of the *turas*. The pilgrim circles sunwise around each station several times while reciting specific prayers, then goes on to the next one.

*Gin* means "to beget, conceive, produce," which brings us back to the mysterious "birth" of the ninth-century definition.

*Tuirigin* is some kind of a traveling, wandering, coursing, encircling birth.

To answer the riddle, I suggest that the "birth" who was never born and never will be is the One Birthing Spirit that has been conceiving, begetting, and engendering us since the beginning of time and will continue to do so until there is no more time. If, of course, there is ever such a time when there is no more time! It's possible that the One Birthing Spirit, let's call it a Mother, will continue to give birth to herself forever, for all eternity.

So there really is only one Great Birth. Call it creation. Call it the shaping of life. Call it the flow of life that passes through each of us, and through everything that is, was, or will be. The poet William Butler Yeats wrote a couple lines that get to the heart of this mystery:

> *The borders of our minds are ever shifting*
> *And many minds can flow into one another...*
> *And create or reveal a single mind, a single*
> *   energy.*[42]

Perhaps we could substitute "soul" for "mind" in this passage and talk about the borders of our souls. They shift. They reach to the ends of the Earth. They flow into one another. And when all is said and done, there is really only One Soul, flowing here and there, summer, autumn, winter, spring. Yes, spring. Springing up as you, as me, as that young tulip in the garden, as that returning robin on the lawn.

# CHAPTER 39

# HEALING THE GREAT SPLIT

In chapter 1 we considered the idea that the four elements and various combinations of them reside in our souls. In fact, they are the soul's very faculties, its powers. In chapter 2 we thought about the idea that the soul's powers extend to the ends of the earth. In the previous chapter we looked at the mystical concept that there is really only One Soul in the entire universe and each of us is part of it.

Try this.

Find some feature in nature that attracts you, something that has a certain beauty or mystery to it. It might be a tree, hillside, garden, a single flower, lake, fallen log, or boulder. But let's say it is a waterfall.

Then go and sit near it, or in some place where you can see it.

Feel its *presence*. In some spiritual traditions, you are asked to "place yourself in the presence of God" before you begin. In this case, you are already in the presence of the waterfall, and you are consciously feeling its presence before you and around you and within you. Sit in this presence and allow it to encompass you for a few moments.

At some point, say to yourself that the presence you feel is the waterfall's *power.* Then sit and absorb that power, noticing what it feels like within you.

Next, acknowledge this power as the *soul* of the waterfall. Again, sit for awhile in this soul space, which is both your own and the waterfall's.

Now the tricky part.

Become aware gradually, in as many ways as you can, or need to, of the Power behind the waterfall's power, the Soul behind its soul, the Shaper behind its shape. Try to feel how this Power or Soul *yearns* to shape the waterfall, and has always yearned to shape it. This Shaping Spirit may have existed even before it was a waterfall. It may be more ancient than the waterfall.

It will continue to shape it or some other waterfall for as long as there is water, stone, height, depth, flow.

Sit with these images and sensations until you feel the great peace that will come over you: the peacefulness that arises when you are one with another creature of beauty and power such as yourself. This is the peace that comes from recognizing and experiencing your oneness with another created being.

Stay in this peacefulness as long as you wish.

When you return from that moment of union, or communion, realize that the reason you can experience this Shaping Power of the waterfall, this Power behind the waterfall, is this: That Power and those Elements are already in you. Both in your body and in your soul.

If there was some Great Split between you and the rest of nature, you would never be able to feel this oneness. But there really is no such Split.

# CHAPTER 40

# Ínvoke Life!

 hen the Gaelic poet Amergin stepped foot on the shores of Ireland, he sang:

*I invoke the land of Ireland:*
*Forceful, the fertile sea;*
*Fertile, the lush highlands;*
*Lush, the showery woods;*
*Showery, the river of waterfalls;*
*Of waterfalls, the lake of deep-pools;*
*Deep-pooled, the hilltop well;*
*Welling, the people of gatherings;*
*Gathering, the tribes of Tara;*
*I invoke the Land of Ireland.*[43]

This book was conceived on the idea that shapes this poem. Namely, that all things are connected, and twine around one another, and weave in and out of the many strands of life. One thing leads to another; everything folds back onto itself and onto all the rest. Nothing stands alone.

Find ways to write poems like this from your own experiences. Write them about places, people, situations, objects, and the events of your life.

Here is one that honors the land where I currently live:

*I invoke the land of this valley:*
*Blossoming, the apple trees on the hill,*
*Hilly, the steep eastern slope,*
*Sloping, the morning sunlight,*
*Sunlit, the clearing of trees,*
*Clear, the winding road,*
*Winding, the stream that flows to the river,*
*Flowing, the seasons of life,*
*Living, these days and nights of home.*
*I invoke this land, this home.*

Write and keep invocations such as these, and add to them. They are simple formulas for celebrating the moments of your life. When you read back through them years from now, they will remind you how your life was connected to places and people and events beyond yourself. From the flowing of line into line, you will recall that nothing is trapped, fixed, permanently set, or isolated forever. Each line, each image, is carried into the next. You may even remember that you wrote these poems because you read this book. And so this book will be woven into your own writing; and you and I, our words and thoughts, will become a tapestry of great beauty.

And so it is with life.

There is always some mysterious wind, shaking the tapestry that veils the mysteries of life. This wind can lift that tapestry. It can lift *you* above the present trouble and carry your soul across the sky.

Where does it come from, this wind? And where does it go?

# ENDNOTES

1.  John Matthews, *Taliesin: Shamanism and the Bardic Mysteries in Britain and Ireland* (London: The Aquarian Press, 1991), p. 54.
2.  John G. Neihardt, *Black Elk Speaks* (New York: Pocket Books, 1975), p. 36.
3.  John Keats, "Letter to George and Georgiana Keats, February 14, 1819," in *The Norton Anthology of English Literature,* Vol. II, (New York: Norton, 1979).
4.  R.J. Stewart, *The Mystic Life of Merlin* (London and New York: Arkana, 1986), p. 212.
5.  Renate Craine, *Hildegard: Prophet of the Cosmic Christ* (New York: Crossroad Publishing Company, 1997), p. 79.
6.  W.H. Gardner, *Gerard Manley Hopkins: A Selection of His Poems and Prose* (Baltimore: Penguin Books, 1964), p. 27.
7.  Mary Low, *Celtic Christianity and Nature: Early Irish and Hebridean Traditions* (Belfast: The Blackstaff Press, 1996), pp. 180–181.

8. Nigel Pennick, *Celtic Sacred Landscapes* (New York: Thames and Hudson, 1996), p. 20.
9. Alexander Carmichael, *Carmina Gadelica: Hymns and Incantations* (Hudson, N.Y.: Lindisfarne Press, 1992), p. 249.
10. Ibid., p. 256.
11. Joseph Campbell, *The Way of the Animal Powers,* Vol. I, (San Francisco: Harper and Row, 1983), p. 169.
12. I Corinthians 3:22–23.
13. John 1:1.
14. Psalms 46:9.
15. e.e. cummings, *100 Selected Poems* (New York: Grove Press, 1959), p. 114.
16. Alwyn Rees and Brinley Rees, *Celtic Heritage: Ancient Tradition in Ireland and Wales* (New York: Thames and Hudson, 1961), p. 128, and Peter Berresford Ellis, *The Druids* (Grand Rapids, Mich.: William B. Eerdman's Publishing Company, 1995), p. 169.
17. Carmichael, *Carmina Gadelica,* p. 198.
18. Ibid., p. 297.
19. Ibid., p. 271.
20. Ibid., p. 217.
21. Ibid, p. 295.
22. Christopher Bamford, *The Voice of the Eagle: The Heart of Celtic Christianity* (Hudson, N.Y.: Lindisfarne Press, 1990), p. 95.
23. Matthews, *Taliesin,* p. 55.
24. Ibid., pp. 296–297.
25. Carmichael, *Carmina Gadelica,* p. 281.
26. Ibid., pp. 379 and 101.
27. Ibid., p. 109.
28. Ibid., p. 337.
29. Ibid., pp. 96–97.
30. Ibid., p. 285.
31. Ibid., p. 621.
32. Ibid., p. 281.
33. Esther de Waal, *Every Earthly Blessing: Celebrating a Spirituality of Creation* (Ann Arbor, Mich.: Servant Publications, 1991), pp. 15–16.
34. Ella Young, *Celtic Wonder Tales* (Edinburgh: Floris Classics, 1988), p. 98.

35. Ibid., p. 81.
36. A.E., *The Candle of Vision: Inner Worlds of the Imagination* (Dorset, England: Prism Press, 1990), pp. 101–102.
37. Ibid., pp. 1–3.
38. Matthews, *Taliesin*, p. 100.
39. De Waal, *Every Earthly Blessing*, pp. 67–68.
40. Ibid., pp. 69–71.
41. John Minahane, *The Christian Druids: On the Filid or Philosopher-Poets of Ireland* (Dublin: Sanas Press, 1993), pp. 137–138.
42. John Sharkey, *Celtic Mysteries: The Ancient Religion* (New York: Thames and Hudson, 1984), p. 24.
43. Matthews, *Taliesin*, p. 54.

# Index

## A

A. E. (George Russell), 150
All-That-Is
  Death and release from
    dualism, 98
  oneness with, 98
Amergin
  boast of, 105–6
  poem, xvii–xviii
  song of, 187
Anima Mundi, Soul of the
  World, 31–32

## B

"Be here now," 160–62
beauty, 79
Beltane, 153–57
  Alaskan, 153–56
  Irish tale of the coldest,
    154–55
  leaping across the fire, 156,
    157
  New York State, 156
Black Elk, xviii–xix
Boudica, 86
body, as elements of nature,
  7–8
Book of Llanrwst, The, 7
Boyne River, Ireland, 25, 26,
  27–28, 29
Braunsberg, Hainburg, Aus-
  tria, 109–11, 115
Brennus, 172–73
Brigid, 113, 131, 142
Buddhism
  Buddha Way, 60
  satori, 65

Bull Hill, Cold Spring, NY,
  9–13

## C

Celtic artwork, xvii, 6
Celtic mythology
  absence of creation myths,
    144–45
  Beltane, 153–57
  Brennus at the Temple of
    Apollo, Delphi, 172–73
  Danu, 26, 110, 113
  gods and goddesses, not in
    human form, 173–74
  Maelduin and the sheep,
    57–58, 60
  Mothers, 41, 113, 141, 150
  nemeton (sacred grove),
    90–93, 97
  Peredur and the quest for
    the Grael, 58, 60
  Young's version, Celtic Won-
    der Tales, 149–50
Celtic poetry
  "boast," 105–6
  ninth-century poem, Cre-
    ator as "King," 176–79
Celtic prayers
  bedtime, 95
  encompassing, "God before
    me," 97
  encompassing, Three of
    Power, 96
  protection, 96
Celtic shamanism, 17, 34
Celtic society
  four directions (airts), 74,
    75–76, 163–65

king, requirements for, 47, 55
King's Truth, 78–79, 81
moral code, 83–87
mysticism, and dualism rejected by, 59–60
question, "Are you still in the forest?," 93
riddle, 179–81
saying, nights on a holy mountain, 115
site, Braunsberg, Hainburg, Austria, 109–11
throwing material wealth into lakes and rivers, 49
warrior's oath, 87
*Celtic Wonder Tales* (Young), 149–50
Cherokee, river in, 25
China, yin-yang in, 59
Chippewa saying, xvii, 150
Christianity
  Anima Mundi, 31–32
  Celtic, early, 136, 137
  encircling prayer, 96
  evangelical, and hostility to pagan religions and shamanism, 167–70
  Jesus, 140–41
  Mary, 130, 131, 179
  Michael (archangel), 130, 131
  Patrick, St., in Ireland and, 135–38, 174
  Roman-style, 136
  Trinity, 140–42
Ciaran, Saint, 37
  prayer attributed to, 40–41
circles, sacred
  between realities and, 91–93
  encompassing with the sacred, 97–98
  protective, 99
Clonmacnoise, Ireland, 36, 40, 75
Cormac, 16–17, 84, 130, 131
courage, 48, 49
Creator, 143–47
  absence of Celtic creation myths, 144–45
  all created things sharing in, 101–2, 137

"boast," creating your own, 107–8
creation as Great Birth, 181
*cruthaitheoir* (creator, shaper), 142
descriptions in Gaelic literature, 175–78
*Dúileamh*, 32, 97, 103
exercise, sharing in creation, 103–4
as "King," 176–79
Sacred Three of creation, prayer to, 146–47
soul sharing in, 107–8, 145
what is creation, 172
cummings, e. e., 70

### D

Danube River, 26
  night-watching on Braunsberg, Hainburg, Austria and, 109–11
death
  as fate, 165
  release from dualism and, 98
  souls after, 20
  truth and, 85–86
Druids, 27
  King's Truth, 78–79
  sanctuaries of, 92–93
  three important things: honor the gods, do no evil, live courageously, 49

### E

Earth (Great Mother), 46, 141
  wind as breathing of, 151
Einstein, Albert, 48, 119
Eskimo god, Sila, 48, 119
Eve, 28
*Evernew Tongue, The*, 6–7
exercises
  asking a river its source, 29
  casting protection around oneself, 99
  facing the directions, 164–65
  healing the Great Split, 183–85
  healing song, 66

letting nature's wonder fill you, 8
listening with your soul, 161–62
observing the "love and affection" of every living thing, 132–33
sharing in creation, 103–4
thinking about the Irish word for Creator, *Dúileamh*, 33
wind, prayers to, listening to, 150–51
writing poems from your own experience, 188–89

# F

faeries, 21–22
    music, 161
    wind, 150
Fairbanks, Alaska, Beltane in, 153–56
fate, destiny, 165
fear, 122–23, 125–26
    incident in Appalachia, "stray sod," 116–19
    night-watching on Braunsberg, Hainburg, Austria, 109–11, 115
    night-watching on Knocknarea, Ireland, 111, 115
    night-watching, Pictish grave, Scotland, 112–13, 115–16
    rupture with the universe into Me and Not Me, and, 122
    as shape-shifter, 121, 123
    soul-making and, 112–13
    vision quest in Catskills and, 121–23
    Zen story of strawberry, 123, 128
flowers, 5–6
forgiveness prayer, 41
*Four Ancient Books of Wales, The*, 3

# G

Galahad, 60
Ganges River, 26

Gaelic
    *airts* (cardinal directions), 74, 75–76, 163–65
    *blath* (prosperity), 164, 173
    blessing, 33
    *caim* (loop, bend), 99
    *craic* (fun), 69
    *cruthaitheoir* (creator), 142
    *deisceart* (southward), 164
    *dúil* and *dúile* (element, created thing, desire, fondness, hope), 32, 97
    *Dúileamh* (Creator), 32, 97, 103
    *dúlra* (nature), 32
    *fidnemed* (forest shrine), 90
    *iarthar* (west), 164
    *nemed* (sanctuary), 90
    *oirhtear* (east), 164, 173
    *tuaisceart* (north), 164
    *tuirigin* (overtaking birth), 180–81
ghosts, 110–12
    Catskill's vision quest and, 121
God
    goodness, love, and yearning and, 102–3, 126
    in heaven or earth (whereabouts of God), 170, 171–74
    Patrick's description of, 175–76
    as shape shifter, 107–8
    silence and, 68, 161
    soul and, 107–8
    surrounding us (encompassing, arms around us), 97–99
    transcendent or immanent, 98, 171, 174, 176
    trinity of divine power and, 137
    word and, 67–68
    *See also* Creator
goddesses, 46
    Triple Goddess, 141
    *See also* Mothers; *specific goddesses*
Gonne, Maud, 44
Grael stories, 58, 60

# H

healing
  music and songs of, 64–65,
    68
  poets, healing and, 64
  spiritual, shamanism as,
    169
  wind, 149–50
Heraclitus, 25
Hildegard of Bingen, 3, 20
holy wells, 35–38
  County Tipperary, moving of
    the water, 35–36
  rules for, 35
  waterless near Clonmac-
    noise, Ireland, honoring,
    36–38
Hopkins, Gerard Manley, 6
Hudson River, 25, 116

# I

Ireland
  author's experience with
    cows on the road in
    Bantry Bay, 51–55
  author's night-watching on
    Knocknarea, 111, 115
  Belfast Waldorf school,
    74–75
  Beltane, tale of the coldest,
    154–55
  cruthaitheoir (creator,
    shaper), 142–43
  daily prayer for strength
    and protection, 135, 137
  Donegal, poetry and song by
    teens, 68–72
  holy wells, 35–38
  Maeve on Irish paper
    money, 43–46
  "medicine wheel" (four di-
    rections, plus center),
    75–76, 77, 78
  myth, three sons of Tuire-
    ann and healing power of
    the wind, 149–50
  prayer, bedtime, 95
  riddle, 179–81
  sacred rivers, 26–27, 29
  saying after a person dies, 86
  St. Patrick in, 135–38
  song of Amergin, 187
  "stray sod," 118
  turas (sacred stations, jour-
    ney around), 180
  See also Gaelic
Irish myth
  Aengus and tale of coldest
    Beltane, 154–55
  Boann, goddess, and cre-
    ation of river Boyne,
    27–28, 63
  Cormac in the Land of
    Truth, 16–17, 84
  Dagda, 63, 64
  directions (airts), 74, 75–76,
    163–65
  Finn MacCool, and "the
    finest music in the
    world," 160, 161
  first stories, 74
  five streams and the Pool of
    Wisdom, 16, 27
  gods of, Tuatha De Danann,
    27
  Lir, god, 27
  Maelduin, 57–58, 60
  Maeve (Queen Maeve,
    Medb), 43–46
  Nechtain, god, 27
  Salmon of Wisdom, 16, 27,
    155
  Shannon, and creation of
    River Shannon, 27
  three harpers, 63–66
  Uaithne, 63, 64
  winds of fate, 73–76

# J

John, Saint, 67–68
Judeo-Christian texts, "fear of
  the Lord," 92

# K

Keats, John, xix
"King," ninth-century poem,
  Creator as 176–79
King's Truth, 78–79

## L

Lenape
  name for Hudson River, 25
  story about Wif-toona-wis,
    monster in the Hudson,
    116
life
  celebrating moments of,
    writing poetry from your
    own experience, 188–89
  charge of, 81
  directions of, 163–65
  response to, controlling, 81
  wheel of, 80–81
  Zen story of strawberry,
    123, 128
Lucan, 92–93

## M

MacCool, Finn, 83, 160, 161
Maeve (Queen Maeve, Medb),
  44–45, 113
  cairn of, Knocknarea, Ire-
    land, 111
  on Irish paper money,
    43–46
  three requirements for a
    husband, 47
Meramec River, Missouri, 116
Mississippi River, 25, 116
moon, blessing, 33
Moses, 92
Mothers, ancestral, 28, 45,
  46, 113, 141
  as Birthing Spirit, 181
  hidden in the land, 43–46,
    179
  prayer for forgiveness, 41
  Triple Goddess, 141
  wind as voice of, 150
  See also Maeve
music
  healing, 64, 65, 66
  Irish story of Finn MacCool,
    and "the finest music in
    the world," 160
  listening exercise, 161–62
  Oran Mór (great song), 112,
    161

of Otherworld, 161–62
  power of, 67
  of the spheres, 65
mystery schools, 101, 103
mystics/mysticism, 16–18
  divine revelation, intensity
    of, 85, 92
  oneness with All-That-Is,
    98, 106
  rejection of dualism, 60
  on souls after death, 20
  See also shaman/shamanism

## N

Navajo
  horzo (Beauty), 79, 81, 97
  prayer, 97
Native Americans, expression
    after a disappointing
    hunt, 40. See also specific
    tribes
nature, xix
  acknowledging (expressing
    gratitude, asking forgive-
    ness) the resources of,
    39–40
  blessings of love from, to,
    Gaelic and Scottish, 33,
    129–32
  body comprised of, 7
  Celtic rejection of dualism,
    59–60
  dualism of Me and Not-Me,
    2, 60, 122
  elements, 3, 5–8
  estrangement from, 135
  exercise, healing the Great
    Split, 183–85
  historic intimacy with, in
    the Highlands, 129–33
  observing the "love and af-
    fection" of every living
    thing, 132–33
  oneness with, 3, 184–85
  perception of, 126–27
  prayer, St. Patrick's,
    "strength of heaven"
    found in, 137, 138, 174
  prayers to spirits of (Scot-
    tish), 131–132

pull of, 8
risk and danger in, 115–19,
126
seasonal rituals, 159
shaman and, 127–28
soul and spirits of, 31, 40
spells, charms, prayers, and
offerings to spirits of, 127
spirits, mischievous or
malevolent, incident in
Appalachia, 116–19
spring and rebirth, 179–81
unpredictability of, 159
nemeton, 90–93, 97
night-watching
Braunsberg, Hainburg, Austria, 109–11, 115
Celtic saying about, 115
Knocknarea, Ireland, 111,
115
Pictish grave, Scotland,
112–13, 115–16
soul-making and, 112–13
nirvana, 65
numbers, magical, 139
threeness, 139–42

# O

oneness with All-That-Is, 98,
106
Oran Mór (great song), 112, 161
Osage people, 26
Otherworld
incident in Appalachia,
"stray sod," 116–19
music of, 161–62
nemeton and, 93
women and, 27–28

# P

Pandora, 28
Patrick, Saint, 83, 135–38
description of God, 175–76
prayer "strength of heaven,"
137, 138, 174
Paul, Saint, 48
peeper toads (tree frogs), 9–13
Peter, Saint, 75
Philip, Apostle, 7

Plato, 101, 141
poetry
author's, invoking the land,
188
Celtic "boast," 105–6
ninth-century, Creator as
"King," 176–79
"this amazing day," 70–71,
72
"Winds of Fate," 73
writing from your own experience, 188–89
Yeats, "borders of our
mind," 181
poets, healing and, 64
prayers
bedtime (Irish, Scottish), 95
blessing (Scottish), 33, 125
blessing for cows (Scottish),
130–31
blessing for seed (Scottish),
131
daily, prayer for strength
and protection, 135, 137
encirclers in, 96
encompassing, "God before
me" (Celtic), 97
encompassing, Three of
Power (Celtic), 96
forgiveness, 41
Gaelic blessing, 33
healing the sick, 66
morning (Scottish), 79–80, 81
to nature (Scottish), 131–132
Navajo, 97
Patrick's, "strength of
heaven," 137, 138, 174
protection (Celtic), 96, 97
runes, sung (Highlands),
130
Sacred Three, prayer to,
146–47
wind, healing prayers and,
151
protection
folk method for casting
power and, around one-
self, 99
prayers (Celtic), 96, 97
Pseudo-Dionysius, 102

# R

Ram Dass, 160
reality
    dualism as illusion, 59–60
    hidden, 46
    as reflective of perception,
        9–13
    as source for mystics,
        15–18
    spiritual dimension of,
        16–18
    story of two hermits, 12
    wind stirring the curtain of,
        150
riddle, 179–81
rivers, 25–29
    danger in, 116
    sacred, as spiritual source,
        26, 28
    *See also specific rivers*
runes, 130, 136

# S

sacred
    circles, 91–92
    terror, fear and, 92, 97,
        112–13
salmon, 19–23, 25–26
Samhain, 20, 21–23
Scotland
    blessing, 33, 125
    blessing for cows, 130–31
    blessing for seed, 131
    Celtic Christians, early, 136,
        137
    historic intimacy with na-
        ture in the Highlands,
        129–33
    morning prayer, 70–80, 81
    night-watching, Pictish
        grave, 112–13, 115–16
    prayer, bedtime, 95
    prayers to nature, 131–132
    runes, 130
    Thomas the Rhymer, 84–85
    tradition, disappearance of,
        133
shaman/shamanism
    Celtic, 17

Christianity's opposition to,
    168–70
defined, 169
honoring the intimacy
    among created things, 128
personal relationship with
    helping spirits, 39
as walker between worlds,
    127–28
*Shaman's Drum* magazine,
    168–69
Shannon River, Ireland, 26,
    29, 36
Sila (Eskimo god), 48
soul, xviii
    Anima Mundi, Soul of the
        World, 31–32
    Creator/God, shared
        essence with, 107–8, 145,
        178
    elements as faculties of, 183
    everything having a spirit, 31
    exercise, healing the Great
        Split, 183–85
    filling, with wonders of na-
        ture, 8
    hidden inside the body, 98
    making, 47–49
    One Soul, 181
    oneness with, knowledge of
        All-That-Is, 106–7
    seven faculties, 3
    surrounding the body and
        infinite, 3–4, 5, 20–21,
        48, 86, 98, 107, 181
sovereignty, 77, 80
    Goddess of, 77
    legend of the brothers and
        the hag, 78
    Maeve as Goddess of, 47
    prayer, 81
spiritual retreats, withdrawal
    from the world, 68, 157
superstition, 99

# T

Taliesin, 3
    boast of, 106
    words on the soul as wind
        voyager, 151

Thomas the Rhymer, 84–85
Thoreau, Henry David, 85
trinity
    of creation (Shaper of Life,
        Shape of Life, Shaping of
        Life), 145–46, 170
    encompassing prayer, Three
        of Power, 96
    of divine power, 137
    Sacred Three, prayer to,
        146–47
    "threeness," 139–42
Truth, 78–80
    consequences of lies, 87
    Cormac in the Land of,
        16–17, 84
    death and, 85–86
    deeper, 85
    discontent and deception,
        85
    right relationship with,
        83–87
    suppression of, 85
    Thomas the Rhymer, 84–85

## U

universe, 7–8
    creation of, descriptions in
        Gaelic literature, 175–78
    exercise, healing the Great
        Split, 183–85
    hostile and malevolent, 119
    loving and affectionate,
        33–34
    question as to the nature of,
        48, 119
    Sila as soul of, 48
    See also nature

## W

Wales and Welsh tradition
    Peredur and the Grail, 58,
        60
    See also Celtic mythology;
        Celtic society
wind
    blessing the newborn child,
        73
    Chippewa saying, xvii, 150
    faery, 150
    healing power of, 149–50
    listening to, 151
    making prayers to, 151
    mystery of, 189
    reality's curtain moved by,
        150
    Taliesin on, 151
    as voice of the goddess, 150
"Winds of Fate," 73
wisdom
    Cormac and the Cup of
        Truth, 84
    of the Otherworld, women
        and, 27–28
word, power of, 67–72

## Y

Yaquina River, Oregon, 19–20
Yeats, William Butler, 44, 181
ying-yang, 59–60
Young, Ella, 149

## Z

Zen story, 123, 128

# About the Author

Tom Cowan is an internationally respected teacher of shamanism, Celtic spirituality, and European mystery traditions. He holds a doctorate in history from St. Louis University, and is the author of *Fire in the Head: Shamanism and the Celtic Spirit; Shamanism as a Spiritual Practice for Daily Life,* and *Wending Your Way: A New Version of the Old-English Rune Poem.* He lives in New York's Hudson River Valley.

To learn more about Tom Cowan, please visit his website at www.riverdrum.com.